TEMPO

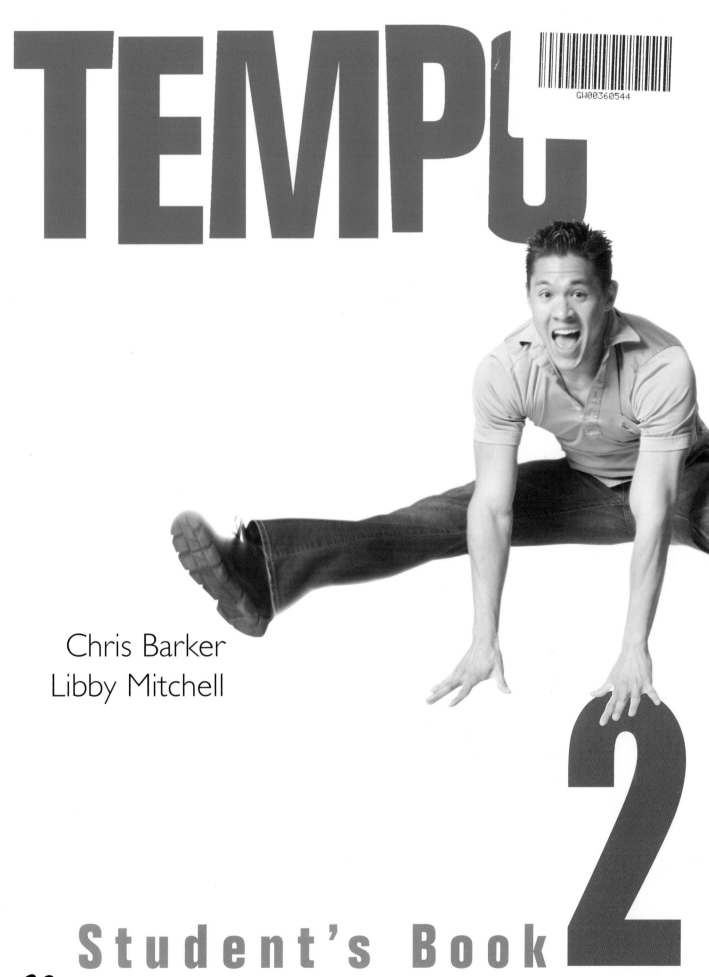

GW00360544

Chris Barker
Libby Mitchell

2

Student's Book

MACMILLAN

Communication Pronunciation	Skills development Culture Spot Portfolio	Workbook Study tips
Describing people's appearance and personality *It's time for (bed).* *It's not fair.* *Stop it!* *It's only (a toy spider).* *Anyway, ...* *It's fun.* *Not for (me).* *Sorry!* /ʃ/	Pets' corner	SB p. 9 ⟶ WB ex. 1–2 SB pp. 10–11 ⟶ WB ex. 4 SB p. 13 ⟶ WB ex. 5–7 SB p. 14 ⟶ WB ex. 8–9 SB p. 15 ⟶ WB ex. 3, 10 Writing in English WB p. 11
Buying things in a shop *Can I help you?* *How much is/are ... ?* *I'd like ... please.* *That's (£1.99), please.* *Thanks.* *Here's your change.* /ʊ/ /uː/	A boy with style Pocket money Write a profile of you, your best friend and a member of your family. Write about your pocket money WB p. 21	SB p. 19 ⟶ WB ex. 1 SB pp. 20–21 ⟶ WB ex. 3–6 SB p. 23 ⟶ WB ex. 7–8 SB pp. 24–25 ⟶ WB ex. 9–13
Making and responding to suggestions *Let's ...* *Why don't we ...?* *I want to ...* /w/	Independence Day	SB p. 33 ⟶ WB ex. 1 SB pp. 34–35 ⟶ WB ex. 3–7 SB p. 36 ⟶ WB ex. 1 SB p. 37 ⟶ WB ex. 8–10 SB pp. 38–39 ⟶ WB ex. 11 Classroom WB p. 33 phrases
Making offers and predictions Expressing decisions Giving advice *(We'll meet) in the usual place.* *It's lovely!* *(I) won't be long.* *You shouldn't swim straight after (lunch.)* *(I'll) just (watch).* Final consonants: /p/ /t/ /k/	Ecology week A trip to Britain Write an e-mail arranging to meet a friend next weekend. Write about yourself. What will you probably do in your next holidays? WB p. 43	SB pp. 43 ⟶ WB ex. 1 SB pp. 44–45 ⟶ WB ex. 4, 5, 7–9 SB pp. 46–47 ⟶ WB ex. 10–12 SB pp. 48–49 ⟶ WB ex. 6, 13

And I'm Alex. We all live in Mill Road.

Hi!

Listen and complete the chart for each person.

Name: Kate Campbell

Age: 13

Family: Mum, Dad, brother

Pets: A hamster called Hercules

Hair: ....

Eyes: ....

Name: Sophie Miller

Age: 12

Family: Mum, Dad, sister

Pets: A cat called Tintin

Hair: ....

Eyes: ....

Name: Ashan Da Silva

Age: 12

Family: Mum, Dad

Pets: —

Hair: ....

Eyes: ....

Name: Alex Jenkins

Age: 12

Family: Mum, Dad, two brothers

Pets: A dog called Bernie

Hair: ....

Eyes: ....

And this is my brother, Jamie. He's really annoying!

Grammar

- Present simple, revision
- *must, mustn't* for obligation and prohibition
- *like* + verb + *ing*
- *be like* (descriptions)
- Verb *let*
- Object pronouns, revision
- *would like* + noun
- *How much is/are ... ?*
- *How much* + noun ...?
- *How many* + noun ...?

Vocabulary

- Physical appearance, revision
- Personality adjectives
- Shops

Communication

Describing people's appearance and personality

Pronunciation

/ʃ/
/ʊ/ and /uː/

Culture spot

Pocket money

1

Physical appearance

1 How many words can you remember in each group?

Height

tall

of medium height

short

Hair length

long

medium length

short

Hair colour

brown

black

fair

blonde

red

reddish-brown

grey

white

Eye colour

 blue

 brown

 grey

 green

Shades of colour

dark (brown)

light (brown)

She's tall.
He's got short hair.
She's got dark brown hair and blue eyes.
He wears glasses.

Personality adjectives

2 Listen and read.

1 She's kind.

2 It's loyal.

3 He's clever.

4 She's patient.

5 He's generous.

6 She's helpful.

7 He's funny.

8 She's sporty.

9 She's shy.

10 He's annoying.

11 She's naughty.

12 He's strict.

3 Think of a person you know for each description. Write their names next to the pictures.

You mustn't do that!

- *must, mustn't* **for obligation and prohibition**
- **Present simple, revision**
- *like* + **verb** + *ing*
- *be like* **(descriptions)**
- **Describing people's appearance and personality**

Listen and read

1 **Listen and read.**

Mum	Jamie, you mustn't do that!
Jamie	It's only water, Mum. And it's fun.
Kate	No, it isn't. Not for us!
Mum	Jamie, you must come in now. It's 8 o'clock. It's time for bed.
Jamie	It's not fair! She always stays up late.
Kate	No, I don't. Anyway, you're only little! [*Jamie squirts Kate with the water pistol.*] Stop it! You're very naughty!
Mum	Jamie!
Jamie	All right, Mum.
Mum	And you mustn't make too much noise.
All	OK, Mrs Campbell. Sorry!

Comprehension

2 **Answer the questions.**

1 What's Jamie's mum called?
   Mrs Campbell

2 Who's in trouble?

3 What's the time?

4 Is it time for breakfast?

5 Who goes to bed first? Jamie or Kate?

Grammar focus

must, mustn't for obligation and prohibition

Affirmative	Negative
I must (come in).	I mustn't
You	You mustn't
He/She/It must	He/She/It mustn't
We must	We mustn't
You must	You ....
They must	They mustn't

Write the missing words.
Look at the dialogue to help you.

What do you notice about *must* and *mustn't*?

Grammar practice

3 **Complete the sentences with *must* or *mustn't*.**

1 I ...must...... do my homework.

2 She mustn't..... stay up late.

3 You .... tidy your room.

4 We .... eat in class.

5 I .... forget my friend's birthday.

6 We .... remember our sports kit.

7 Jamie .... go to bed now.

8 Kate and her friends .... make too much noise.

4 Complete the caption for each picture.
What must they do?

eat the birthday cake ~~make too much noise~~
go to bed have a shower
clean the kitchen

1 You mustn't make too much noise.

2 Mum, we ....

3 You naughty dog! You ....

4 You ....

5 I ....

5a Listen. Then act out this scene.

Mum	It's time for bed.
Sam	It's not fair!

Sam	Stop it!
Chloe	It's only a toy spider. Anyway, it's fun.
Sam	Not for me!
Chloe	Sorry!

5b Complete the dialogues then act them out.

Mum	.... to do your homework.
Sam	.... !

Chloe	.... !
Sam	.... a balloon.
	....
Chloe	.... !
Sam	.... !

1

Read

6 Read about the children.

My name is Kate.

School: Finchley Girls' School

Sports: swimming and football

Favourite food: everything!

My name is Alex.

School: Hampstead Boys' School

Sports: football, rugby, swimming and tennis

Favourite food: everything!

My name is Ashan.

School: Hampstead Secondary School

Sports: athletics, swimming

Favourite food: Chinese food

My name is Jamie.

School: Mill Road Primary School

Sports: football, basketball, cricket, swimming, rugby, tennis

Favourite food: pizza, chocolate,

I don't like vegetables or salad. Yuck!

My name is Sophie.

School: Hampstead Secondary School

Sports: tennis, swimming

Favourite food: pasta, fruit

Listen

7 Who is talking? Write the names in the order they speak.

1 ..Jamie..........   4 ....

2 ....   5 ....

3 ....

Grammar focus

ℝ Present simple

Affirmative

I/You/We/They like   (chocolate).
He/She/It likes

Negative

I/You/We/They don't like   (cheese).
He/She/It doesn't like

Questions and short answers

Do I/you/we/they like   (chocolate)?

Yes, I/you/we/they do.
No, I/you/we/they don't.

Does he/she/it like   (chocolate)?

Yes, he/she/it does.
No, he/she/it doesn't.

Remember!

He/She/It   go**es**, do**es**, ha**s**

Grammar practice

8 Complete the questions and answers.

1 Which school ....**does**....... Kate go to?

She .....**goes**........ to Finchley Girls' School.

2 .... she play football?

Yes, she ....

3 .... she play rugby?

....

4 What's her favourite food?

She .... everything.

5 .... her brother .... vegetables?

No, he ....

Speak

9a Work with a partner.

Partner A: Ask about Kate and Sophie.
Partner B: Ask about Ashan and Jamie.

A Which school does Kate go to?

B She goes to Finchley Girls' School.

A Does she play football?

A Does she go swimming?

A What's her favourite food?

A Which school does Sophie go to?

A Which sports does she like?

A What's her favourite food?

B Does Ashan go to Jamie's school?

B Does Ashan go swimming?

B What's his favourite food?

B Which sports does Jamie like?

B Which school does he go to?

B Does Jamie like all kinds of food?

Ask Partner B a question about Alex.
Ask Partner A a question about Alex.

9b How much can your partner remember?
Give clues like this:

A He likes chocolate.

B That's Jamie.

A They play tennis.

A She goes to a girls' school.

🎧 Read and listen

10a Choose a caption for each picture.

2 ....

1 I like playing on my computer. ....

I like ...	reading in bed.	going to my friends' houses.
	shopping.	listening to music.
	riding my bike.	playing on my computer.
	playing outside with my friends.	watching TV.
	surfing.	

3 ....

10b Listen and check.

Grammar focus

like + verb + ing
I like reading in bed.
He likes riding his bike.
She likes listening to music.

 (Remember!) dance   dance+ing   dancing
ride   ride+ing   riding

11 Grammar practice

Use the verbs in the brackets to complete the sentences.

1 She likes .....skating... (skate)
2 I like .... stories about animals. (read)
3 I like .... football. (watch)
4 We like .... up late. (stay)
5 We like .... to the beach. (go)
6 I don't like .... (dance)

Speak

12a Work with a partner. Talk about what Kate, Jamie, Sophie and Ashan like doing.

Partner A: Talk about Kate and Jamie.
Partner B: Talk about Alex and Ashan.

 A Kate likes surfing.

12b Tell your partner what you like doing. Is there anything you don't like doing?

Extra!

12c Tell your partner what your best friend likes and doesn't like doing.

Write

13 Write four sentences about what your partner likes and doesn't like doing.

Martha likes playing on her computer. She ....

doesn't like doing her homework...........................

4 ....

Be careful!

What's she **like**?   She's very nice./She's quite tall.
What does she **like**?   She likes music and sport.

Match the answers to the questions.

1 What does he like   He's clever and he's quite shy.
   doing?
2 What does he like?   He likes playing on his
                            computer.
3 What's he like?   He likes chocolate.

Pronunciation

/ʃ/

16a **Listen and repeat.**

1 shy   4 shower
2 short   5 patient
3 she   6 nationality

16b **Listen again and underline the /ʃ/ sound.**

Listen and read

14 **Listen and read.**

My mum is patient and helpful.
My dad is strict but he's very kind.
My brother is often naughty but he's very funny.
I'm shy but I'm quite sporty.

Comprehension

15 **Choose two sentences to describe the photo.**

Speak

17 **Talk about your family and friends using the
words in the box.**

kind	clever	shy
annoying	helpful	strict
funny	naughty	patient
loyal	sporty	generous

A What are your grandparents like?

A What's your best friend like?

B My grandparents are very generous.

B My best friend is loyal and
   he is also very funny.

18 **Write a paragraph about your family
and friends.**

My grandparents live in Portugal. My grandmother
is quite short. She's got reddish- brown hair and
green eyes. She wears glasses. She's patient and
very generous. She likes reading and she also
likes going to football matches. My grandfather
is ...

Pets' corner

Read

1 **Read about the pets.**

Tell us about your pet, send in a photo and win a prize!

Name
Gemma

Personality
She's very clever.

 playing with her toys

Name
Tess

Personality
She's loyal and very patient.

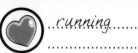 ..running.......

 ..spiders......

Name
Herbert

Personality
He's quite shy.

 eating..........

 .cats............

Name
Pip

Personality
He's quite naughty and very funny.

 sitting on my bed, watching TV

 Loud music

Speak

2 Find a word or phrase in the text for each picture.

5 Work with a partner, ask and answer questions about the pets.

1 ...sitting on my bed............

> **A** What's Gemma like?

> **B** She's clever.

> **A** What does she like?

2 ....

> **B** She likes playing with her toys and hiding. She doesn't like cuddles.

3 ....

> **B** What's Tess like?

> **B** What does she like?

Write

4  ....

6 Write a profile of Floppy the rabbit, using the pictures.

5 ....

6 ....

Name
Floppy

Personality
clever, quite sporty

Read

3a Find the meaning of these words and phrases in a dictionary, or ask your teacher.

		Find
1	cuddles	cuddle (*noun*)
2	long walks	walk (*noun*)
3	loud noises	noise
4	cameras	camera
5	having a bath	bath (*noun*)
6	barking	bark (*verb*)
7	hiding	hide (*verb*)

3b Guess where the words and phrases in Exercise 3a fit in the pets' descriptions. Write them in the gaps.

Listen

4 Listen and check your answers to Exercise 3b.

His name is Floppy. He's ....

Let's check

Vocabulary check

1 **Complete each sentence with the correct word.**

annoying	clever	funny	generous	helpful
loyal	~~naughty~~	patient	shy	sporty	strict

Don't eat my dinner, you .....**naughty**..... cat.

1 I'm quite .... I help my mother a lot with the cleaning.

2 He always gets 100% in Maths. He's very ....

3 She's very .... She's in the tennis, swimming and athletics teams.

4 His aunt is very .... She always gives him £100 for her birthday.

5 We always laugh when we're with Joey. He's very ....

6 We can't start yet so please be .... for another ten minutes.

7 He's like a mouse. He's very .... and he never comes out of his room.

8 Her parents are very .... She can't go to parties, she can't watch TV on weekdays and she can't stay up late at weekends.

9 He's very .... He never says bad things about his brother.

10 This computer game is .... It stops after ten minutes.

Write your score: .... /10

Grammar check

2 **Choose the correct form of the verb.**

You (must) / mustn't listen to me! This is important.

1 You *must* / *mustn't* eat sweets in class.

2 You *must* / *mustn't* go to bed now. It's really late.

3 You *must* / *mustn't* stay up late. There's a big match tomorrow morning.

4 You *must* / *mustn't* tidy your room. It's a mess.

5 You *must* / *mustn't* eat my chocolates, you bad dog!

Write your score: .... /5

3 **Choose the correct word for each sentence.**

I ...**do**..... athletics at my school.

A does   (**B** do)   **C** doing

1 .... school does your brother go to?

A Where   **B** When   **C** Which

2 I don't like .... in cold water.

A swim   **B** swims   **C** swimming

3 " .... he like?" "He's really funny."

A What   **B** What's   **C** Is

4 My mother .... wear glasses.

A doesn't   **B** isn't   **C** don't

5 .... you live in London?

A Are   **B** Does   **C** Do

6 She always .... to music in bed.

A listens   **B** listening   **C** listen

7 You mustn't .... your homework.

A forget   **B** to forget   **C** forgetting

8 What .... your cat like eating?

A do   **B** does   **C** is

9 "Do you like your school?" "Yes, ... "

A I like   **B** I do   **C** it is

10 "What is she like?" " .... "

A Funny.   **B** Reading.   **C** Music.

Write your score: .... /10

4 **Make sentences by putting the words in order. Add capital letters where necessary.**

bed / breakfast / having / in / likes / mum / my
My mum likes having breakfast in bed. ....

1 the phone / do you / friends / like / on / talking / your / to / ?

....
....

2 doesn't / doing / her / homework / like / Maths / my / sister

....
....

3 are / Canadian / cousins / like / what / your / ?

....
....

4 and watching / biscuits / dog / eating / likes / my / videos.

....
....

5 computer / we all / and listening / like / games / to / music.

....
....

Write your score: .... /5

Write your total score: .... /30

2 Shops

1 Listen and point to the shops. 🎧

2a Write the name of each place.

The Shopping Centre

1 café........... 2 .... 3 ....

4 .... 5 ....

Food Shops

6 ....bakery........ 7 ....

8 .... 9 .... 10 .... 11 ....

2b Work with a partner. Ask and answer to check.

A What's number 1?

B It's a café. What's number 2?

3 Talk about the shops in your town.

A There's a chemist's in Park Street. It's next to the bank.

B There's a newsagent's near my house. It's called One Stop.

Mum doesn't let me do anything

- **Verb** *let*
- **Object pronouns, revision**
- *would like* + **noun**
- *How much is/are* ...?
- *How much* + **noun** ...?
- *How many* + **noun** ...?

Listen and read

1 **Listen and read.**

Sophie	How much money have you got, Kate?
Kate	I've got ten pounds. How much have you got?
Sophie	I've got about fifteen.
Kate	OK, do you want to go shopping this afternoon?
Sophie	Great idea!
Kate	Mum, can I go shopping this afternoon?
Mum	On your own?
Kate	No, with Sophie. I need some things for school.
Mum	Well, all right then. But you must be back by 5.30.
Kate	OK.
Jamie	That's not fair. Mum lets you go shopping. She doesn't let me do anything.
Ashan	Never mind, Jamie. Shopping's boring.
Alex	Shopping's for girls!

Comprehension

2 **Answer the questions.**

1 Who's got fifteen pounds? ....Sophie......................
2 Has Kate got any money? ....
3 Where does Kate want to go? ....
4 Why does Kate want to go shopping?.................
5 Can Jamie go shopping?.....................................
6 Do Ashan and Alex like shopping? ....

Grammar focus

let + object pronoun + verb

We don't let her go shopping on her own.

They don't let me go shopping on my own.

I let him stay up till 8.00.

She lets me stay up till 8.00.

Subject pronoun	Object pronoun
I	me
you	you
he	him
she	her
it	it
we	us
you	you
they	them

Grammar practice

3 Complete the sentences with the verb *let* and an object pronoun.

1 **Mum:** I let Kate stay up till 10.30.
   Kate: Mum _lets me_ .... stay up till 10.30.

2 **Dad:** I let Sophie go shopping with her friends.
   Sophie: Dad .... go shopping with my friends.

3 **Daniel:** I don't let my sister come into my room.
   Sister: He .... go into his room.

4 **Mum and Dad:** We don't let Luke and Maisie go surfing on their own.
   Luke and Maisie: They .... go surfing on our own.

5 **Rebecca:** My mum lets me use her computer.
   Mum: I .... use my computer.

6 **Jenny:** I don't let my mum and dad read my diary.
   Mum and Dad: She .... read her diary.

7 **Sam:** My mum doesn't let me choose my clothes.
   Mum: I .... choose his clothes.

8 **Lauren and George:** Our cousins let us swim in their pool.
   Ben and Emma: We .... swim in our pool.

Listen

4 Listen and complete the chart.

Speak

5 Work with a partner. Use the chart in Exercise 4. Ask and answer about Sophie and Ashan.

> **A** Do Sophie's parents let her stay up late at the weekend?

> **B** Yes, they do. Do Ashan's parents let him stay up late?

Extra!

6 Work with a partner. Talk about what your parents let you do.

stay up late
buy my own clothes
go shopping with my friends
ride my bike on the road
go to school on my own
buy sweets
watch TV in the morning
surf the internet
go swimming with my friends
have friends to stay
cook

> **A** My parents let/don't let me stay up late at the weekend.

> **B** My parents never/sometimes let me stay up late.

Sophie	✓		
Ashan			

Vocabulary

7 **Write the names of the shops.**

A bookshop

B ....

C ....

That's expensive!

D ....

Speak

9 **Work with a partner. Ask and answer about the shops in Exercise 8.**

A What's your favourite clothes shop?

B Where do you buy your books?

A Which music store do you go to?

B Where do you buy presents for your friends?

Listen

8 **Listen and tick (✓) the shops Kate and Sophie visit.**

1 chemist's	....	**7** supermarket	....
2 newsagent's	....	**8** department store	....
3 bookshop	....	**9** jeweller's	....
4 music store	....	**10** sports shop	✓..
5 clothes shop	....	**11** café	....
6 shoe shop	....	**12** bakery	....

10 **Listen and read.**

Assistant	Can I help you?
Kate	I like those little animals. How much are they?
Assistant	They're four pounds each.
Sophie	Oh, that's good. They're really sweet.
Kate	The pink pig's nice.
Sophie	How many pigs have you got? You don't want another one!
Kate	I've only got twelve. Anyway, you know I collect them. Excuse me, I'd like one of the animals, please.
Assistant	Which one would you like?
Kate	I'd like the pink pig, please.
Assistant	That's four pounds, please. Thanks. Here's your change.
Kate	Thanks.

Comprehension

11 **Answer the questions.**

1 What does Kate like in the shop?
   She likes the little animals.
2 What does Sophie think of them?
3 Does Sophie think the animals are expensive?
4 Which one does Kate want to buy?
5 Why does Sophie say: 'You don't want another one!'?
6 Who buys the pig?

Grammar focus

would like + noun
I'd like one of the animals, please.
Which one **would you like?**
I'd like the pink pig.

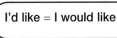
I'd like = I would like

Grammar practice

12a **Complete the dialogue between a waiter and a customer in a café.**

Waiter	What ..would.............. you like?
Customer	.... like a sandwich, please.
Waiter	What .... you .... in your sandwich?
Customer	.... like ham and cheese.

12b **Now role-play another dialogue in a café.**

cheese

chicken

ham

salami

tuna

salad

tomato

Extra!

13 **Listen and answer the questions.**

1 What are Alex and Ashan doing?
   They're shopping.
2 How much money has Ashan got?
3 What does he want to buy?
4 How many football stickers can he get for two pounds?
5 Who do Alex and Ashan meet?

Talk time

14 **Listen and complete the dialogue.**

Assistant	Customer
Can......... I help you?	Yes. How much .... that pencil case?
It's seven pounds fifty.	And how much .... those pens?
They're one ninety-nine each.	.... like two pens, please. A red one and a black one.
That's three pounds ninety-eight, please. Thank you. Here's your change.	....

Grammar focus

How much is/are...?
How much? How many?

How much is that pen?
How much are those sunglasses?

How much money have you got?
How much water do you drink every day?

How many euros have you got?
How many glasses of water do you drink at lunchtime?

Complete the rules.

We use *how* .**much**. when we ask about prices in a shop.

We use *how* .... with uncountable nouns, like *bread, milk* and *sugar*.

We use *how* .... with countable nouns like *bananas, books* and *pens*.

Speak

15 **Work with a partner. Role-play similar dialogues about these things.**

A Can I help you?

B Yes, how much is that T-shirt?

A It's £11.99.

B And how much are those sweatshirts?

1

£11.99

£18.50

2

£7.50

55p each

3

£1.50

£10

4

£8.50

£69.99

Grammar practice

16 **Complete the questions with *how much* or *how many*. Then answer them.**

1 ..How much...... is an ice cream?
2 .... brothers and sisters have you got?
3 .... time do you spend watching TV?
4 .... subjects do you study at school?
5 .... are your favourite sweets?
6 .... languages do you speak?

17a **Listen and repeat.**

/ʊ/	/uː/
book	you
butcher	fruit
would	supermarket

17b **Listen and add these words to the correct column.**

17c **Listen and check.**

Read and speak

18 **Answer the questions about yourself. Then ask your partner.**

Healthy Lifestyle Survey

Every day ...

1 How much water do you drink?

2 How much fruit do you eat?

3 How many sweets do you eat?

4 How many times do you brush your teeth?

5 How many hours do you sleep?

Every week ...

6 How many times do you play or do a sport?

7 How much do you spend on fizzy drinks?

8 How many pizzas do you eat?

9 How much time do you spend outside?

10 How much time do you spend watching TV?

Write

19 **Write the questions in this interview with Homer Simpson.**

1 How many sports do you play? ....
I don't play any sports.

2 ....
I eat 20 doughnuts every day.

3 ....
I spend 10 hours a day watching TV.

4 ....
I don't drink water.

5 ....
I've got 10 dollars and you can't have it!

6 ....
I've got two, a cat and a dog.

Portfolio

20 **Write a profile of you, your best friend and a member of your family. Go to page 128.**

	You	Your partner

Skills development
A boy with style

 Listen

1 Listen and complete the information.

Name	Max Pearmain ....
Age	....
Lives	in Norwich, England.
Family	Mum, Dad, two .... Rosie (9), Lily (.........)
Pets	....
Hobbies	.... and collecting things.

'I like being different.'

Read

2 Read about Max and tick (✓) the chart.

Max is a boy with style. He likes clothes and he likes shopping. But his parents don't let him have a lot of money, so on Saturday afternoons he works in a designer clothes shop in Norwich. He gets £10 for 3 hours.

Max doesn't spend a lot of money on clothes but he collects designer bags and adverts from magazines and he sticks them on the wall in his room. He's got a lot of things in his room but it's very tidy. He likes showing his room to friends. But he doesn't let his little sisters play in it!

	True	False	Don't know
1 Max is sporty.			✓
2 His parents give him a lot of money.			
3 He works in a music store.			
4 He likes collecting things.			
5 He puts pictures on his walls.			
6 He lets friends watch TV in his room.			
7 Rosie and Lily sometimes play in his room.			

4 **Write questions for these answers.**

1 What ..does he like doing in his room...............?

He likes doing his homework, reading and listening to music.

2 Has ....?

Yes, he has, but he doesn't often watch it.

3 What ....?

A Muji bike.

4 What ....?

It's very stylish.

5 How ....?

£200.

6 What ....?

All sorts of things.

🎧 Listen and read

3 **Listen and read.**

I really like my room. I like doing my homework, reading or listening to music here. I've got a bed, a sofa, a desk, a computer, a television and a CD player. I don't watch much TV but I like listening to music.

I want to buy a Muji bike. It's Japanese and it's very stylish. It costs £200. That's twenty Saturdays at the shop!

I collect all sorts of things as you can see. I like being different.

Speak

5 **Work with a partner. Talk about your room. Use these questions to help you.**

- Do you like your room?
- What's it like? What have you got in it?
- Is your room tidy?
- Do you let other people come into your room? Who?
- Do you put anything on your walls? What kind of things?
- Do you do your homework, read or listen to music in your room?
- Do you watch TV in your room?
- Is there something special you want to buy? What is it? How much does it cost?
- Do you collect anything? What do you collect? How many have you got?

I like my room. It's not very big but there's a bed, a cupboard for my clothes ...

Write

6 **Now write about your room.**

My room is small but I like it. I've got ....

Culture spot

Pocket money

🎧 Listen and read

(1) **Listen and read.**

How much pocket money do you get?
What do you spend it on?

> I don't get pocket money, but my mum gives me some money when I tidy my room, clean the bathroom, or help in the kitchen. She doesn't let me spend it all. She says I must save some for my holidays.
>
> *Lydia*

> I get £3.50 a week. I buy CDs with my pocket money. My sister gets £5. I don't think it's fair. She says she's 14 and I'm only 12, so it is fair!
>
> My grandparents give me money for my birthday. They're very generous.
>
> *Josh*

Comprehension

(2) **Who:**

1 has got a sister?
Josh ....

2 has got a brother?
....

3 gets £12 a week?
....

4 sometimes works in a shop?
....

5 helps in the house?
....

6 likes music?
....

7 doesn't spend all his/her money?
.... and ....

8 likes shopping?
....

I'm 13. I get £4 a week from my parents and I do a paper round, too. I get £8 a week for that. I spend some of it on magazines or sweets, but I always save £2 a week.

My brother is 8. He gets £2 a week from my parents, but when he's naughty he doesn't get anything. They're quite strict!

Niall

I don't get pocket money. My parents have got a shop. They give me some money when I help them. And I get money for my birthday from my uncles and aunts. When I've got some money, I go into town to buy clothes. I like spending money!

Anita

Speak

3 **Are you like any of the people in the interviews? Say why.**

I'm like	Josh	because	I buy CDs with my money.
	Lydia		I don't get pocket money.
	Niall		my mum gives me money.
	Anita		I help in the house.
			I always save £2 a week.
			I help in my parents' shop.
			I get money from my uncles and aunts.
			I like spending money.
			I buy my own clothes.

I'm like = I'm similar to

I'm like Josh because I buy CDs with my pocket money.

Vocabulary

4 **Make a list of things you spend your money on. Find the words you don't know in a dictionary.**

Write

5 **Now write about your pocket money.**

Let's check

Vocabulary check

1 **Match the places to the clues.**

bakery	fruit and vegetable shop	newsagent's
café		record shop
~~cinema~~	hairdresser's	sports shop
department store	jeweller's	supermarket

You can see a film here. .cinema.....................................

1 You can buy your new CDs here. ....

2 Get your apples and bananas here. ....

3 Come to this big shop for clothes, books, shoes, jewellery and other things. ....

4 You can get fish, cheese, chocolate, milk and fruit here. ....

5 Come here for your newspapers and magazines. ....

6 Have coffee, juice or sandwiches here. ....

7 You can buy a watch or a bracelet here. ....

8 You can buy bread and cakes in this shop. ....

9 They cut and wash hair in this place. ....

10 You can buy a tennis racket here. ....

Write your score: .... /10

Grammar check

2 **Choose the correct words for each sentence.**

My brother's 16. My parents let ..him.. stay up late.
A her   **(B him)**   **C** it

1 Those are my shoes. You can't wear ....
A it   **B** that   **C** them

2 How .... money have you got with you?
A much   **B** many   **C** is

3 We're really late. Can you take .... in the car?
A we   **B** our   **C** us

4 What .... like?
A you would   **B** would you   **C** you

5 Please let .... go to the party.
A I   **B** you   **C** me

6 That's Maria's sister. Do you like ....?
A him   **B** her   **C** it

7 How .... tickets have you got?
A much   **B** many   **C** are

8 How .... are the stickers?
A much   **B** many   **C** long

9 'Would you like a drink?' 'Yes, ...'
A I like   **B** please   **C** it is

10 I always let my cat .... on my bed.
A sleep   **B** sleeping   **C** to sleep

Write your score: .... /10

3 **Choose the correct words for each sentence.**

I would like to/a sandwich, please.

1 How *much/many* are the apples?

2 Luigi's parents let him *ride/to ride* his bike to school.

3 How many *sticker/stickers* can I get for 5 euros?

4 How *much/many* time do you spend watching TV?

5 My parents never let me *staying/stay* up till eleven o'clock.

Write your score: .... /5

4 **Complete the dialogue with *would like* or *'d like*.**

B What ..would... you ....like..... to drink, Maria?

A I'**(1)** .... apple juice, please.

B They haven't got apple juice. **(2)** ....
you .... some orange juice?

A No, thanks. Can I have a lemonade?

B OK. And what **(3)** .... you
.... to eat?

A I'**(4)** .... an ice cream.

B Chocolate, coffee or vanilla?

A I **(5)** .... a coffee ice cream,
please, Dan.

Write your score: .... /5

5 **Write sentences by putting the words in order. Add capital letters where necessary.**

cousins / got / have / how / many / you / ?
How many cousins have you got?.....................

1 at / late / let / me / My / parents / stay / the / up / weekend.
....
....

2 blue / how / is / much / sweatshirt / the / ?
....
....

3 choose / clothes / do / let / own / parents / you / your / your / ?
....
....

4 does / drink / how / hamster / much / water / your/ ?
....
....

5 does / father / how / languages / many / speak / your / ?
....
....

Write your score: .... /5

Write your total score: ... /35

How good are you?

★ I'm not very good at this. ★★ I'm OK at this. ★★★ I'm good at this.

Tick (✓) the correct boxes.

		★	★★	★★★
READING I can understand:				
people saying what others must/mustn't do	*You must come in now.*			
questions and answers about people's personality	*What's he like? He's clever.*			
words on a plan of a shopping centre	*chemist's, jeweller's, hairdresser's*			
a simple survey	*How many hours do you sleep?*			
LISTENING I can understand:				
simple statements about daily life	*I go to Mill Road Primary School. I play tennis.*			
questions and answers about prices	*How much are they? They're £1.50 each.*			
a simple interview	*What are your hobbies, Max? I like shopping and collecting things.*			
information about someone's lifestyle	*Max doesn't spend a lot of money on clothes.*			
questions and answers about pocket money	*How much pocket money do you get, Josh?*			
WRITING I can write:				
about what people must/mustn't do	*We mustn't forget our sports kit.*			
about what people like/don't like doing	*We like going to the beach. I don't like dancing.*			
about what people let/don't let others do	*I don't let my mum and dad read my diary.*			
about my room	*My room is small but I like it.*			
SPEAKING I can:				
ask and answer questions about daily life	*Which school does Kate go to? Which sports does Jamie like? Does Ashan go swimming?*			
ask and answer questions about someone's personality	*What's your best friend like? My best friend is loyal and he's also very funny.*			
name different kinds of shops	*There's a chemist's in the centre.*			
talk about rules at home	*My parents let me have friends to stay.*			
ask simple questions about shopping	*Where do you buy presents for your friends?*			
ask prices and pay for things in shops	*How much are those sunglasses? I'd like two pens, please.*			
describe my bedroom	*I like my room. It's not very big.*			
talk about pocket money	*I get £3.50 a week.*			
say who people are like	*I'm like Anita because I don't get any pocket money.*			

Vocabulary groups

Write three more words in each vocabulary group.

Physical appearance	tall	blue eyes	....	....	....
Personality adjectives	kind	annoying	....	....	....
Shops	chemist's	butcher's	....	....	....

Grammar

R Present continuous, revision
Present continuous for future use
Future with *going to* + verb
want to + infinitive
Let's ...
Why don't we ...?
Future with *will* for offers, predictions and decisions
should
Possessive pronouns

Vocabulary

Weather
Parts of the body
Action verbs

Communication

Making and responding to suggestions
Making offers
Giving advice
Expressing decisions

Pronunciation

/w/
Final consonants: /p/ /t/ /k/

Culture spot

A trip to Britain

Why don't we go to the beach?

3

Weather

1 **Listen and number the pictures.** 🎧

It's cold. ☐

It's warm. ☐

It's cloudy. 1

It's windy. ☐

It's hot and sunny. ☐

It's foggy. ☐

It's snowing. ☐

It's raining. ☐

There's going to be a storm.
Listen to the thunder.
Look at the lightning. ☐

2 **What's the weather like today?**

What are we doing at the weekend?

Wild Woods

- Present continuous for future use
- Present continuous, revision
- Future with *going to*
- *want to* + infinitive
- *Let's ...*
- *Why don't we ...?*
- Making and responding to suggestions

Listen and read

1 Listen and read.

Kate What are we doing at the weekend, Mum?

Mum I'm going shopping on Saturday morning, Dad's doing the garden ...

Kate So you aren't doing anything special.

Mum No, not really.

Kate Well, why don't we go karting at Brands Hatch?

Mum It's a long way.

Jamie Let's go to a theme park. What about Legoland?

Mum No, Jamie. It's expensive.

Kate I know! Why don't we go to Holkham Beach? They're having a carnival there this weekend.

Jamie Oh, yes! Mum, can we go?

You can use *they* to mean people generally:
***They**'re having a carnival this weekend.* = *There's a carnival this weekend.*

Comprehension

2 Match the person to the activities.

1    a

c

2    b

3    c

4    d

Grammar focus

Present continuous for future use

Affirmative	Negative
I'm going.	I'm not staying.
You're going.	You aren't staying.
He's/She's/It's going.	He/She/It isn't staying.
We're/You're/They're going.	We/You/They aren't staying.

Questions	Short answers	
Am I going?	Yes, I am.	No, I'm not.
Are you going?	Yes, you are.	No, you aren't.
Is he/she/it going?	Yes, he/she/it is.	No, he/she/it isn't.
Are we/you/they going?	Yes, we/you/they are.	No, we/you/they aren't.

You can use the Present continuous to talk about future plans:

What are you doing this weekend?
(= What are your plans for the weekend?)
I'm seeing friends.

R You can also use the Present continuous to talk about what is happening now:

What are you doing?
I'm reading.

Grammar practice

3 **Respond using the prompts.**

1 go to the cinema   ✗
    play football   ✓

Can I come to the cinema with you on Saturday?

I'.m.not.going.to.the.cinema..I'm.playing.........
...football..

2 go to the beach   ✓
    study for an exam   ✗

Let's go to the beach with them at the weekend.
They ....

....

3 make a cake   ✓
    make a big pizza   ✗

I can help you make a cake for Mark's birthday.

I ....

....

4 have a party   ✗
    go to a theme park   ✓

Are you going to Lucy's party next Friday?
She ....

....

5 play tennis   ✗
    go out   ✓

See you at the tennis courts at 7 this evening!
Oh, sorry, we ....

....

Listen

4 **Listen and answer the questions.**

1 Who does Kate phone first? .....Sophie.................

2 Is Sophie busy at the weekend?........................

3 What are Kate and her family doing at the weekend?..

4 What are Ashan's plans for the weekend?

....

5 What does Ashan decide to do? ....

6 Can Alex go to the beach?..............................

Speak and write

5a **Work with a partner. Ask and answer about plans for the weekend then tick (✓) the correct column.**

> **A** Are you going shopping at the weekend?

		Yes	No
1	go shopping		
2	play football		
3	go swimming		
4	go for a bike ride		
5	go to the beach		
6	go to the cinema		
7	stay at home		
8	do anything special (What?)		

5b **Tell another pair of students about your partner's plans for the weekend.**

> **B** Carla is going shopping on Saturday afternoon. She's going to the beach on Sunday.

5c **Write what the other students are doing at the weekend.**

Carla and Mark are going shopping.....................
Isabel is going to the cinema.............................

6 **Write about your plans for the weekend.**

On Saturday morning I'm going riding. In the
afternoon I'm meeting my friends in town.......

3

 Read and listen

7a **Choose a sentence for each picture.**

a It's cloudy.   e It's snowing.
b It's cold.   f It's warm.
c It's foggy.   g It's windy.
d It's raining.   h It's hot and sunny.

2 ....

3 ....

4 ....

1 ....

7b **Listen and check.**

Listen and read

🎧 **8** **Listen and read.**

> *Kate and Sophie are talking on the phone.*
> *They're packing their bags for the weekend.*
>
> **Kate** I'm going to take jeans, a jumper, a T-shirt ...
>
> **Sophie** Are you going to take a dress?
>
> **Kate** No, I'm not.
>
> **Sophie** What are you going to wear for the carnival?
>
> **Kate** My wetsuit.
>
> **Sophie** What! It isn't going to rain all weekend!
>
> **Kate** No, I know. It's going to be hot and sunny. But I'm going to go as a shark.
>
> **Sophie** Well, I'm going to take my swimsuit.
>
> **Kate** Your swimsuit?
>
> **Sophie** Yes, but I'm not going to go swimming. I'm going to go to the carnival as a mermaid.
>
> **Kate** Well, watch out for the sharks!

Comprehension

9 **Find a word in the dialogue for each picture.**

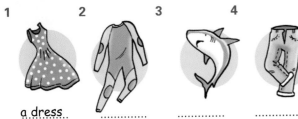

1	2	3	4
a dress	....	....	....

5	6	7	8
....	....	....	....

Grammar focus

Future with *going to*

I'm/You're/He's/   **going to** (take a T-shirt).
She's/It's/We're/
You're/They're

You can use *going to* to talk about intentions:

She isn't going to take a dress.
Is she going to take a wetsuit? Yes, she is./No, she isn't.

You can also use *going to* to talk about something that is likely to happen:

Look at those clouds. It's going to rain.

Grammar practice

10 **Complete the sentences.**

Affirmative

1 I'm going to...... meet my friends in town this afternoon. Do you want to come?

2 They .... have a pizza. Let's go with them.

3 'We .... go on a school trip to Russia.' 'That's fantastic!'

4 Let's go to the beach on Saturday because it .... be hot and sunny.

Negative

5 I'm tired. I'm not going to... play football tonight.

6 We .... watch TV because we've got a lot of homework.

7 You don't need an umbrella. It .... rain.

8 They're losing 1-3. They .... win.

11 **Complete the sentences with *going to* and the phrases in the box.**

not/go swimming	work in a zoo
~~join a club~~	wear jeans
not/watch TV this evening	be cold

1 I want to play tennis more often so I 'm going to.. join a club.....

2 He likes animals so he ....
   ....

3 Don't forget your jumper. It ....
   ....

4 The sea's very cold so they ....
   ....

5 I've got a lot of homework. I ....
   ....

6 Sophie and Kate aren't going to take dresses. They ....

12 **Complete the questions.**

1 .Are... you .going to.. invite him to your party?

2 What .... you .... wear for the party?

3 ' .... they .... see the new *Star Wars* film on Saturday?' 'No, they aren't.'

4 ' .... she .... visit her pen-friend next year?' 'Yes, she is.'

3

13 **Listen and read.**

Comprehension

14 **Write the name of a person for each picture.**

Ashan	What are we going to do when we get there?
Sophie	Let's go to the beach!
Alex	Why don't we have the picnic first?
Kate	I want to go surfing.
Ashan	I want to go canoeing.
Mum	Well, I want to put the tents up. And guess what? You're all going to help me!

1

.....Ashan..............

2

....

3

....

4

....

5

....

Grammar focus

want to + infinitive

Affirmative
I want to go.

Negative
I don't want to go.

Questions
Do you want to go?

Grammar practice

15 **Match the sentences.**

1 It's hot today.
2 Do you want to play tennis?
3 It's my birthday next week.
4 It's snowing.
5 We're going to go ice skating.
6 I don't want to watch that video again.

a I want to go out and make a snowman.
b It's boring.
c Do you want to come?
d I want to go to the beach.
e I want to have a party.
f No, thanks. I'm tired.

You can use *Let's* and *Why don't we* to make suggestions about what you'd like to do.

Let's eat the cake now. I'm hungry.
Why don't we watch a video? There's nothing interesting on TV.

Talk time

16 **Work in groups of four or more. Use the table to talk about what you want to do next weekend.**

Let's ...	go swimming.	go to the cinema.
	go surfing.	watch TV.
Why don't we ...?	have a picnic.	go shopping.
	go for a bike ride.	go karting.
I want to ...	play football.	

Extra!

17 **Write your group's dialogue. Then act it out.**

 ## Pronunciation

/w/

18 **Listen and repeat.**

1	warm	6	why
2	windy	7	want
3	weather	8	wear
4	weekend	9	where
5	what	10	watch

Speak and write

19 **Work with a partner. Look at the map. Ask and answer about the weather at the weekend. Then write about the weather.**

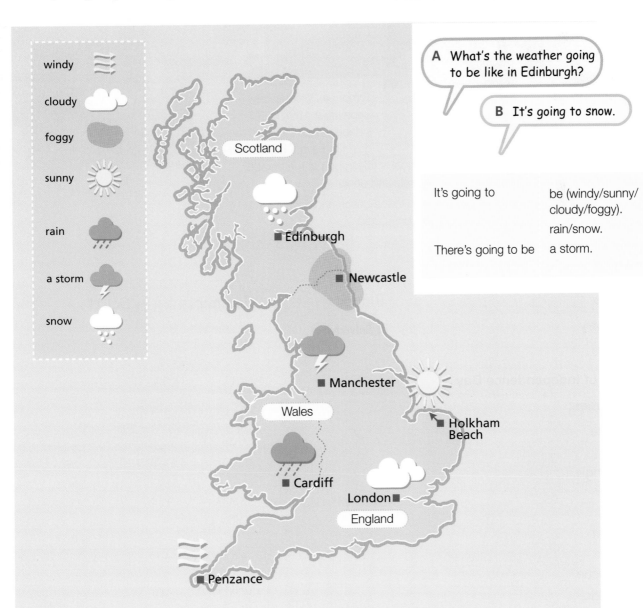

A What's the weather going to be like in Edinburgh?

B It's going to snow.

It's going to	be (windy/sunny/ cloudy/foggy).
	rain/snow.
There's going to be	a storm.

Skills development

Independence Day

Read

1 **Read about Independence Day in El Salvador and in Ukraine. Complete the chart for Blanca and Vladimir.**

El Salvador

Tomorrow, Wednesday September 15th, is Independence Day. We're going to have a big parade in San Salvador, our capital city. My school is taking part in the parade. We're going to play musical instruments and dance.

After the parade, we're going to drive to the beach and have a party. And we aren't going to go to school on Thursday.

Blanca

Name	Blanca	Vladimir	Scott
Country	El Salvador		
City			
Date of Independence Day			
Activities:			
parade	✓		
party			
dancing			
music			
circus			
market			
beach			
barbecue			
fireworks			

Ukraine

2 Listen to Scott talking about Independence Day in his country and complete the chart.

Speak

3 Work with a partner. Talk about what Blanca, Vladimir and Scott are going to do on Independence Day.

Write

4 Write a paragraph about how Scott is going to celebrate Independence Day.

Scott's going to go to a parade, and then ....

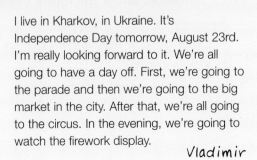

I live in Kharkov, in Ukraine. It's Independence Day tomorrow, August 23rd. I'm really looking forward to it. We're all going to have a day off. First, we're going to the parade and then we're going to the big market in the city. After that, we're all going to the circus. In the evening, we're going to watch the firework display.

Vladimir

Let's check

Vocabulary check

1 **Complete the missing letters in the weather words.**

c <u>o</u> <u>o</u> l

1 cl _ _ _ y
2 w _ _ _ y
3 f _ _ _ y
4 s _ _ w _ _ g
5 l _ _ h _ n _ _ g

6 s _ _ _ y
7 r _ _ n _ _ g
8 c _ _ d
9 h _ _
10 w _ _ m

Write your score: .... /10

Grammar check

2 **Write sentences about the future using the Present continuous.**

(I/play) tennis on Saturday with Julie.
I'm playing tennis on Saturday with Julie.

1 (Lily/come) to the party on Friday.

....

....

2 What (you/do) this weekend?

....

....

3 (We/not go) to the beach tomorrow.

....

....

4 (Who/make) dinner tonight?

....

....

5 My cousins (not leave) on Tuesday morning.

....

....

Write your score: .... /5

3 **Write sentences about the future using *going to*.**

(they/camp) in France or (they/stay) in a hotel?
Are they going to camp in France or are they going to stay in a hotel?

1 (you/watch) the match on TV?

....

....

2 What (you/say) to your parents about the computer?

....

....

3 How long (you and your family/be) in Canada?

....

....

4 Go away you silly dog. I (not/give) you a sweet.

....

....

5 Lucy's brother (study) in Spain next year.

....

....

Write your score: .... /5

4 **Choose the correct words for each sentence.**

What ..<u>are you</u>... doing after dinner?
A you   B you are   **C are you**

1 Do you want .... swimming tomorrow?
A going   B go   C to go

2 We .... tennis at four o'clock.
A plays   B playing   C are playing

3 She .... going on the school skiing trip in December.
A isn't   B doesn't   C don't

4 Why .... we meet at the beach?
A aren't   B don't   C are

5 Let's .... to the carnival this weekend.
A go   B going   C to go

6 When are you going .... to Dave?
A write   B to write   C writing

7 .... going to do my homework tonight.
A I'm not   B I not   C I don't

8 What time .... going shopping?
A she's   B does she   C is she

9 .... we stay at home and watch TV?
A Let's   B Why are   C Why don't

10 .... Joe and Ben coming to your party?
A Are   B Do   C Is

Write your score: .... /10

Write your total score: .... /30

4

Parts of the body

1 Listen and read. 🎧

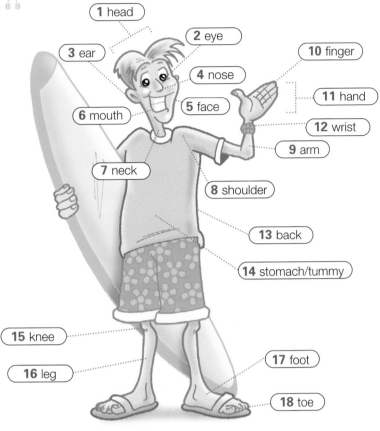

1 head
2 eye
3 ear
4 nose
5 face
6 mouth
7 neck
8 shoulder
9 arm
10 finger
11 hand
12 wrist
13 back
14 stomach/tummy
15 knee
16 leg
17 foot
18 toe

 The plural of *foot* is *feet*.

Action verbs

2 Listen and do the actions. 🎧

Stand up straight.

Click your fingers.

Stamp your feet.

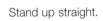

Clap your hands.

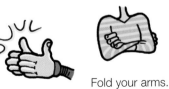

Fold your arms.

Touch your toes.

3 Now tell your partner to do the actions. You can say them in any order.

4 Listen and do the actions. 🎧

Touch your head
Touch your knees
Touch your toes.

Touch your back
Touch your ears
Touch your nose.

Stand up straight
Fold your arms
Stamp your feet.

Clap your hands
Click your fingers
And repeat.

Touch your head
Touch your knees
Touch your toes.

Touch your back
Touch your ears
Touch your nose.

Stand up straight
Fold your arms
Stamp your feet.

Clap your hands
Click your fingers
That's neat!

4

I'll carry the picnic basket

- **Future with** *will* **for offers, predictions and decisions**
- *should*
- **Possessive pronouns**
- **Making offers**
- **Giving advice**
- **Expressing decisions**

 Listen and read

1 **Listen and read.**

Near Holkham Beach.

Mum	Here we are.
Alex	I'll carry the picnic basket.
Kate	I'll take the football and my surfboard. It'll be great for surfing today.
Mum	Take your fleeces and jackets. It'll be cold and windy on the beach.
Kate	No, it won't. It's a lovely sunny day.
Mum	I'll go and park the car in the car park. I won't be long.
Kate	OK, Mum, we'll see you on the beach.
Mum	Where will you be?
Kate	We'll be in the usual place, near the sand dunes.

Comprehension

2 **Answer the questions.**

1 Where are Kate and her friends?
  They're near Holkham Beach.
2 Who wants to go surfing?
3 What's the weather like now?
4 Where is Kate's mum going?
5 Do they often go to this beach? How do you know?

44

Grammar focus

Future with *will* for offers, predictions and decisions.

Affirmative

I/You/He/She/It/We/You/They'**ll** (go).

Negative

I/You/He/She/It/We/You/They **won't** (go).

Questions	**Short answers**
Will I/you/he/she/it/we/you/ they (go)?	Yes, I/you/he/she/ it/we/you/they will.
	No, I/you/he/she/ it/we/you/they won't.

Affirmative 'll go = will go
Negative won't go = will not go

Use the future with *will* for:

offers	I'll carry the picnic basket.
predictions	It'll be cold and windy on the beach.
decisions	I'll go and park the car.

Grammar practice

(3a) Complete the sentences with *'ll* or *won't*.

1 You ..'ll.. be cold.
Take a jumper.

2 I .... answer it.

3 He's friendly. He
.... bite.

4 Don't take the
umbrella. It
.... rain.

5 We ....
catch the 11.30
train.

(3b) Complete the questions and short answers with the correct form of *will*.

1 A ......Will........ Brazil win the World Cup?
B Yes, they ......will.........!

2 A .... you be home late tonight?
B No, I ....

3 A .... they see their cousins at the weekend?
B Yes, they ....

4 A .... Anna be at the concert tonight?
B Yes, she ....

(4) Complete the dialogues with *'ll* or *will* and the correct verb from the box.

take	have	~~carry~~	not/get	make
not/go	help	snow	record	

1 'These surfboards are heavy.'
'It's OK, I.'ll carry........... one of them.'

2 'I can't do my science homework.
'...................... you .... me?'
'Yes, of course.'

3 'I'm going out. I'll miss my favourite programme.'
'Don't worry, I'll ask Dad. He .... it for you.'

4 'We're late!'
'Right, we .... a taxi'

5 'It's cold today.'
'We .... to the beach.'

6 'It's Anna's birthday tomorrow.'
'I .... her a cake.'

7 'I want to go to the concert.'
'No chance. You .... a ticket.'

8 'We're going to the south of Spain in the summer.'
'Fantastic! You .... a really good time.'

9 'Look, it's raining. No skiing tomorrow!'
'I'm sure it .... tonight.'

Speak

(5) Work with a partner. Role-play dialogues using the prompts.

1 A I'm hungry.
B (*Offer to make him/her a sandwich.*)

> B I'll make you a sandwich.

2 A I can't do my homework.
B (*Offer to help.*)

3 A I'm thirsty.
B (*Offer to get him/her a drink.*)

4 A Emma's arriving on Saturday evening.
B (*Offer to meet her at the airport.*)

5 A We need a goalkeeper for Saturday.
B (*Offer to play.*)

4

Listen and read

6a Before you read, listen and underline the parts of the body you hear.

arm	fingers	hands	knee	stomach
<u>wrist</u>	foot	head	legs	toes

6b Listen and read.

Sophie   Come on, let's go in the sea!

Mum   You should put some sunscreen on first, Sophie.

Alex   It's cold!

Kate   No, it's not. It's lovely!

Ashan   Are you coming in, Mrs Campbell?

Mum   No, thanks. I'll just watch.

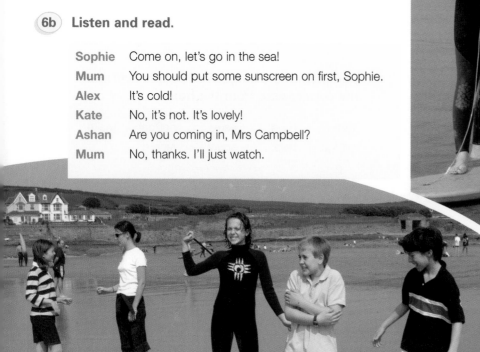

Kate   Put the strap round your wrist. Hold onto the board with both hands. Lie with your stomach flat on the board. Keep your legs straight. Point your toes.

Ashan   Great! We'll go in again straight after lunch!

Mum   No, you shouldn't swim after a meal, Ashan.

Alex   I can't feel my fingers. They're white.

Kate   Stop moaning, Alex, and have a sandwich.

Comprehension

7 Put the pictures in the order of the dialogue.

a ☐
b ☐

c 1
d ☐

Grammar focus

should

Affirmative

I/You/He/She/It/We/You/They   should (go).

Negative

I/You/He/She/It/We/You/They   shouldn't (go).

Questions		Short answers	Affirmative
Should	I/you/he/she/it/ we/you/they (go)?	Yes, I/you/he/she/it we/you/they	should.
			Negative
		No, I/you/he/she/it we/you/they	shouldn't.

You use *You should* + infinitive to give advice.

46

Grammar practice

8 Complete the sentences with *should* or *shouldn't*.

Stay safe in the sea and the sun

1 You **shouldn't** swim straight after lunch.

2 You .... always wear a hat in the sun.

3 You .... never look at the sun.

4 You .... always wear sunglasses to protect your eyes.

5 You .... swim alone.

6 You .... sit in the sun when it's very hot.

7 You .... wear a T-shirt for water sports.

8 You .... drink lots of water on hot days.

9 You .... leave pets in the car on hot days.

10 You .... put more sunscreen on after swimming.

Speak

9 Work with a partner. Respond to what your partner says using *should/shouldn't* with a verb from the box and practise these dialogues.

> eat   come   spend   tidy   stay up   ~~open~~

1 **A** It's hot in here.

  B You ......**should open**.......... the window.

2 **B** She's always hungry at school in the morning.

  A She .... a good breakfast.

3 **A** He's always tired on Monday mornings.

  B He .... so late on Sunday night.

4 **B** Mum, my room's a mess. I can't find anything.

  A You .... it.

5 **A** They've never got any money.

  B They .... it all on sweets.

6 **B** We're not doing anything this weekend.

  A You .... with us on a bike ride.

Extra!

10 Work with a partner. Look at the completed leaflet in Exercise 8 for 30 seconds. Close your books and try to remember the 10 sentences.

Talk time

11a Listen and repeat.

1 (We'll meet) in the usual place.

2 It's lovely!

3 I won't be long.

4 No, you shouldn't swim straight after a meal.

5 I'll just watch.

11b Work with a partner. Choose a sentence for each speech balloon. Then practise the dialogues.

1
'See you later.'
'I won't be long'.

2
Come and have a fight!

3
Bye. See you in Africa.

4
Can I go in now, Mum?

5

4

Before you read

12 **Look at the picture and answer the questions.**

1 Where are they?
2 What are they doing?
3 Is it breakfast time, lunchtime or dinnertime?

Listen and read

13 **Listen and read.**

Kate	Which is my potato? Is that one mine?
Alex	No, that's yours.
Kate	But it's hard.
Alex	It'll be ready soon. Stop moaning!
Ashan	Mmm, my sausage is really good.
Sophie	Ours are burnt.
Kate	Yes, they are.
Alex	I'll have yours.
Kate	No, you won't. Hands off! Oink, oink!
Mum	That's enough.

What are Kate and her friends cooking?

Grammar focus

Possessive pronouns

Subject pronouns	Possessive adjectives	Possessive pronouns
I	my	mine
you	your	yours
he	his	his
she	her	hers
it	its	its
we	our	ours
you	your	yours
they	their	theirs

Find the possessive pronouns in the dialogue which stand for:

my potato	----->	..........mine..........
your potato	----->	....
our sausages	----->	....
your sausages	----->	....

Grammar practice

14 **Rewrite the sentences in italics, replacing the underlined words with possessive pronouns.**

1 I've got my swimsuit. *Where's <u>your swimsuit</u>?*
   Where's yours?.....
2 My hands are cold. *Are <u>your hands</u> cold?*
3 Those are your sunglasses.
   <u>My sunglasses</u> are here.
4 'Is this your surfboard?'
   'No, it's <u>her surfboard</u>.'
5 'Is this your car?'
   'No, it's <u>their car</u>.'
6 'Are your sausages good?'
   'No, <u>our sausages</u> are burnt.'
7 'Is this our football?'
   'No, it's <u>his football</u>.'

Pronunciation
Final consonants: /p/ /t/ /k/

15 **Listen and repeat.**

/p/	/t/	/k/
1 stamp	5 foot	9 neck
2 clap	6 jacket	10 bike
3 stop	7 straight	11 black
4 cup	8 won't	12 stomach

Speak

16 Work with a partner. Ask and answer about the things in your pictures.

> **A** My dog's black and white. What colour's yours?

> **B** Mine's brown. My bike's red. What colour's yours?

Partner A	Partner B
My things	My things

1
2
3
4
5
6

17 Write about your things and your partner's things.

	Me	**My partner**
dog	Mine's black and white.	His/Hers is brown.
bike		
school bag		
trainers		
jacket		
pencil case		

> Urgh! Whose trainers are these?

> Whose trainers are these?
> or
> Whose are these trainers?

Speak

18 Work in groups of three or four. One person in each group puts two or three objects into a bag. Another member of the group takes an object out of the bag and asks:

> Whose (pen) is this?

Members of other groups try to guess:

> It's Alexandra's.

Portfolio

19 Write an e-mail arranging to meet a friend next weekend. Go to page 129.

Skills development

Ecology week

I go to Northgate High School. It's Ecology Week. I'm cycling to school to save energy and to keep the air clean.

Read

1 **Read and match the rules to the pictures.**

Ecology Week Rules

1 We will close doors and windows to keep the classrooms warm. `e`

2 We will switch off lights when we leave the room. ☐

3 We will turn off the TV and the computers when we aren't using them. ☐

4 We will put on jumpers when it's cold. ☐

5 We will not waste water. ☐

6 We will not drop litter. ☐

7 We will recycle paper and cans. ☐

8 We will not go by car when we can walk, cycle or take the bus. ☐

Listen

2 Listen and tick (✓) the chart.

	Switch it off!	🚲	🚶	KEEP THIS SCHOOL TIDY	♻
Charlie				✓	
Ailsa					
Joshua					
Lauren					
Thomas					

Speak

3 Work with a partner. Talk about the things you can do to improve the environment at your school.

A We'll make a garden.

A We won't drop litter.

We'll	make	a garden
We won't	drop	chewing gum in the bin
	put	lights on
	use	litter
	recycle	our bikes to get to school
	turn off	paper and cans
	leave	recycled paper
		the computers

Write

4 Make a poster to show how you can improve the environment at your school.

We'll recycle paper and we'll ...

4 Culture spot

A trip to Britain

Read

1 Read about the places in Britain.

You're planning a trip to Britain with your family or your school. Where will you go? What will you do?

You'll probably arrive in London. Why don't you take a bus trip to see the sights?

Cornwall is in the south-west of England. It's usually warm and sunny there. There's a path along the coast which is open to everybody. You can walk for miles. You can also swim and go surfing.

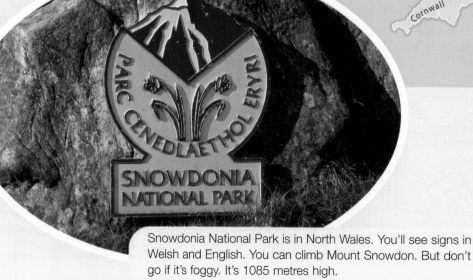

Snowdonia National Park is in North Wales. You'll see signs in Welsh and English. You can climb Mount Snowdon. But don't go if it's foggy. It's 1085 metres high.

Spend a few days in the Lake District. It often rains here, so it's very green. There are lots of campsites where you can stay. And you can take a boat trip on Lake Coniston. The boat is a steam boat but it's called 'The Gondola'!

Visit Loch Ness in Scotland. It's a big lake. Perhaps you'll see the Loch Ness Monster! In the winter it's cold and it snows. You can go skiing or snowboarding in the mountains.

York is in the north of England. It's an ancient city with a beautiful cathedral. You can still see the Roman walls. People say there are ghosts after dark there. You can visit the museums and then you can go shopping for presents to take home.

Comprehension

2 **Where is it?**

a

Scotland

b

....

c

....

d

....

3 **Where can they go?**

1 'I love mountains. My hobby is climbing.'
  .Wales......
2 'I want to go snowboarding.'
3 'Why don't we go to the beach?'
4 'I like historical places.'
5 'I don't like beach holidays or visiting cities. I prefer camping in the countryside.'
6 'Let's go on an open-top bus and see Buckingham Palace and Big Ben.'

Vocabulary

4a **Work with a partner. Read the text again and try to guess the meaning of these words.**

1	sights	6	trip
2	path	7	steam boat
3	coast	8	ancient
4	miles	9	cathedral
5	Welsh	10	ghosts

4b **Check your answers in a dictionary or with your teacher.**

Write

5 **Work in groups. Make a guide to your country for visitors of your age.**

You'll probably arrive in .... You can visit the cathedral. Then you ....

Let's check

Vocabulary check

1 **Complete the sentences with the correct words.**

> back ~~arms~~ ears eyes feet fingers
> hands head mouth shoulders stomach

Dogs and cats have four legs. They don't have .arms. .

1 Open your .... What can you see?

2 We hear with our ....

3 Have you got chewing gum in your ....? No, I'm eating a sweet.

4 You've got big .... What size shoes do you wear?

5 Lie on your .... Look at the sky.

6 In a passport photo you only see a person's .... and ....

7 We've got ten .... on our ....

8 Don't have another fizzy drink. It's bad for your ....

Write your score: .... /10

Grammar check

2 **Complete the conversations with *will*, *'ll* or *won't* and a verb from the box.**

> eat have ~~be~~ play give make

What time .....**will**..... you .....**be**...... home?

1 'We're going skiing this winter.'
'Lucky things! You .... a fantastic time.'

2 'Can I give your hamster a crisp?'
'He .... it. He doesn't like crisps.'

3 'I'm really tired.'
'Sit down, Mum, and I .... you a cup of tea.'

4 'I haven't got any money.'
'Dad .... you some.'

5 Can I use your computer? I .... any games. I just want to send an e-mail.

Write your score: .... /5

3 **Choose the correct words for each sentence.**

'I can't find my bike.' 'You can use ..**mine**....'

A I'm **B** my **C** mine

1 What are you doing with that diary? It's not ......

A you're **B** yours **C** your

2 What time ..... be back?

A will you **B** are you **C** are you going

3 ...... carry your bag.

A I'm **B** I **C** I'll

4 'Let's meet at ten.' 'OK. See you at ten. .... be late.'

A I don't **B** I won't **C** I'll

5 These are our CDs. ...... are in the blue box.

A Theirs **B** They're **C** There's

6 'I can't find the letter from Mark.'
'You ...... tidy the mess on your desk!'

A will **B** should **C** want

7 'Will Poland win the match?' 'Yes, ...'

A they'll **B** they will **C** they're going

8 .... be there at four o'clock.

A We **B** We'll **C** We're

9 I've got a lot of homework. ....
watch TV tonight.

A I shouldn't **B** I don't **C** I'm not going

10 'Let's go for a swim.' 'No, you ....
swim after a big meal.'

A won't **B** aren't **C** shouldn't

Write your score: .... /10

4 **Write sentences by putting the words in order.**

at / look / shouldn't / sun / the / You
You shouldn't look at the sun.......................

1 aren't / green / mine / sunglasses / Those

....
....

2 are / cheese / not / ours / sandwiches / theirs / These

....
....

3 bag / carry / for / I'll / picnic / the / you

....
....

4 back / on / put / should / some / sunscreen / You / your

....
....

5 call / me / morning / in the / time / What / will / you / ?

....
....

Write your score: .... /5

Write your total score: .... /30

How good are you?

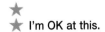 ★ I'm not very good at this.  ★★ I'm OK at this. ★★★ I'm good at this.

Tick (✓) the correct boxes.

		★	★★	★★★
		★	★★	★★★

READING I can understand:

a simple dialogue about future plans	*I'm going to go to the carnival as a mermaid.*			
a simple article about Independence Day celebrations	*We're going to have a big parade.*			
a list of ecology rules at a school	*We will recycle paper and cans.*			
a brochure about sightseeing in Britain	*Visit Loch Ness in Scotland. It's a big lake.*			

LISTENING I can understand:

a phone conversation about weekend plans	*Hi, Ashan, are you doing anything at the weekend?*			
people talking about things that are going to happen	*It's raining. There's going to be a storm.*			
someone talking about celebrations for Independence Day	*There's going to be a big firework display in Central Park.*			
a conversation about safeguarding the environment	*I'll cycle to school. I won't come in the car.*			

WRITING I can:

write about fixed plans	*She isn't having a party. She's going to a theme park.*			
write simple advice for summer holiday safety	*You shouldn't swim alone. You should drink lots of water on hot days.*			
complete a chart about my things compared with my partner's	*Mine's red. Hers is blue.*			
write sentences for a poster about intentions to improve the environment	*We won't leave lights on.*			
write a brochure about sightseeing in my country	*You'll probably arrive in ... . You can visit the cathedral.*			

SPEAKING I can:

describe the weather	*It's cool. It's cloudy. It's raining.*			
ask and answer questions about definite future arrangements	*Are you doing anything special at the weekend?*			
make suggestions for next weekend	*Let's go swimming. Why don't we have a picnic? I want to play football.*			
use a weather map to talk about what the weather is going to be like	*What's the weather going to be like in Edinburgh? It's going to snow.*			
make offers with *'ll*	*I'll make you a sandwich.*			
give advice using *should/shouldn't*	*She should eat a good breakfast.*			
compare objects using possessive pronouns	*Your jacket's red. Mine is blue.*			
make decisions to improve the environment	*I'll cycle to school next week.*			

Vocabulary groups

Write five more words in each vocabulary group.

Weather	thunder	foggy	....	....	....	....	....
Parts of the body	wrist	shoulder	....	....	....	....	....

Module 3

Grammar

Comparatives and superlatives of adjectives

too + adjective

not + adjective + *enough*

Past simple of *be*

Past simple of regular verbs

Past time adverbials: *last Saturday, the day before yesterday, yesterday morning/lunchtime/evening*

I'm the best player.

Vocabulary

Geographical features

Points of the compass

Television programmes

Communication

Making comparisons

Talking about the past

Pronunciation

Final consonants: /g/ and /d/

Past simple endings: /t/ /d/ /ɪd/

Culture spot

Guides and Scouts

Geographical features

1 **Listen and read.** 🎧

1 sea

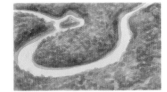

2 river

3 waterfall

4 lake

5 field

6 track

7 mountain

8 mountain range

9 rainforest

10 cave

11 desert

12 island

13 volcano

2 **Work with a partner. Match the names below to the geographical features.**

El Yunque	9	the Nile	
Everest		the Sahara	
Niagara Falls		Constance	4
Cyprus		Etna	
the Alps		the Mediterranean	

Points of the compass

3 **Listen and read.** 🎧

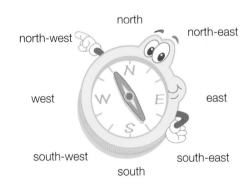

north
north-west   north-east
west   east
south-west   south-east
south

4 **Name a city in your country at each point of the compass.**

... is in the north.

5

The highest mountain

- Comparatives and superlatives of adjectives
- *too* + **adjective**
- *not* + **adjective** + *enough*
- **Making comparisons**

Listen and read

1 **Listen and read.**

Jamie	I'm 1 metre 27. How tall are you?
Alex	I'm 1 metre 52.
Jamie	It's easy for you. You're taller than me.
Alex	I know, but I'm older, Jamie. I'm 12. You're only 7.
Jamie	Kate's 13 and she's taller than you.
Kate	I'm 1 metre 63. I'm the tallest. And I'm the best player!
Alex	We'll see about that!

Comprehension

2 **Complete the chart.**

	Jamie	Alex	Kate
Height	1.27 m		
Age			

Grammar focus

Comparatives and superlatives: short adjectives

Adjective	Comparative	Superlative
tall	taller (than)	the tallest
short	shorter (than)	the shortest
big	bigger (than)	the biggest
small	smaller (than)	the smallest
old	older (than)	the oldest
young	younger (than)	the youngest
large	larger (than)	the largest

To make the comparative of an adjective, add *er:*
You're tall**er than** me.

If the adjective ends in e, you only add *r:*
large → large**r**

To make the superlative of an adjective, add *est:*
I'm **the** tall**est**.

If the adjective ends in e, you only add *st:*
large → the large**st**

Note:

bi**g**	bi**gg**er (than)	the bi**gg**est
hot	ho**tt**er (than)	the ho**tt**est
dry	dr**i**er (than)	the dr**i**est

Grammar practice

3 **Complete the sentences with the comparative or superlative form.**

1 Jamie is 1 metre 27. He's (short) ...<u>shorter</u>... than Alex.

2 Kate is 1 metre 63. She's (tall) .... than Jamie.

3 Alex is 12. He's (young) .... than Kate.

4 Alex is 1 metre 52. He's (short) .... than Kate.

5 Kate's 13. She's the (old) ....

6 Jamie's 7. He's the (young) ....

4a Read questions 1–8 in the quiz and choose the answers. Then listen and check.

? ? ? ? ? ? ? QUIZ ? ? ? ? ? ? ?

1 Is the USA bigger than Canada?
  a Yes, it is.
  b No, it isn't.
  c They're the same size.

2 Is England smaller than Russia?
  a Yes, it is.
  b No, it isn't.
  c They're the same size.

3 Which is colder, Greenland or Russia?
  a Greenland
  b Russia

4 Which desert is larger?
  a The Kalahari
  b The Sahara

5 Which river is longer?
  a The Amazon
  b The Danube

6 Which mountain is higher?
  a Everest
  b K2

7 Which place is hotter?
  a Mali, Africa
  b Iraq, in the Middle East

8 Which city is older?
  a London
  b New York

9 Which is the biggest country in the world?
  a Russia
  b China
  c India

10 Which is the smallest country?
  a Luxemburg
  b Monaco
  c Vatican City

11 Which is the largest lake?
  a The Caspian Sea
  b Lake Michigan
  c Lake Superior

12 Which is the longest mountain range?
  a The Alps
  b The Andes
  c The Rocky Mountains

13 Which is the deepest ocean?
  a The Pacific
  b The Atlantic
  c The Arctic

14 Where is the driest place on earth?
  a The Atacama Desert in South America
  b The Sahara Desert in North Africa
  c The Gobi Desert in Central Asia

15 Where is the highest active volcano in the world?
  a It's in Russia.
  b It's in Chile.
  c It's in Japan.

16 Which is the highest waterfall?
  a Yosemite, in California, USA
  b Tugela, in South Africa
  c Angel Falls, in Venezuela

17 Which city has the largest population?
  a Los Angeles
  b Bombay
  c Mexico City

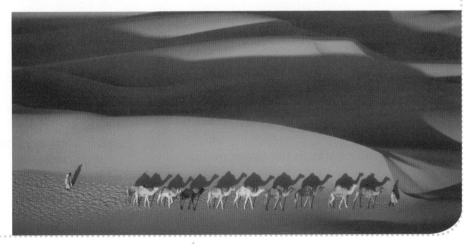

Extra!

4b Now answer questions 9–17. Then listen and check your answers.

5 Work with a partner. Ask and answer the quiz questions.

5

Sophie	Which is the most popular sport in Italy?
Ashan	That's easy! Football!
Sophie	Which is the most beautiful city? That's Venice.
Ashan	Oh, I don't think so. Florence is more beautiful than Venice.
Sophie	Is Britain as big as Italy?
Ashan	No, Italy's bigger.
Sophie	Yes, I think so, too. Which is the most famous building in Rome?
Ashan	The Colosseum. Remember the film *Gladiator*?
Sophie	Where are the best beaches?
Ashan	Hang on a minute. I'll check. In Sardinia. Look, it's an island, off the west coast.
Sophie	Oh yes. Is the north of Italy more industrial than the south?
Ashan	Mmm, I don't know.
Sophie	Which is better, pizza or pasta?
Ashan	That's not on the worksheet.
Sophie	I know, but I'm hungry!

Comprehension

7　**Find the names in the dialogue for:**

1　two countries ..Britain, Italy....
2　three cities
3　a famous building
4　an island
5　three compass points
6　a sport
7　two things to eat

Grammar focus

Comparatives and superlatives: longer adjectives

To make the comparative, put **more** before the adjective.
To make the superlative, put **the most** before the adjective:

| popular | **more** popular (than) | **the most** popular |
| important | **more** important (than) | **the most** important |

Many two-syllable adjectives follow the same rule:

famous　　　more famous　　　the most famous
(also: boring, patient, careful)

Adjectives ending in **y** change the **y** to **i** and add **er** or **est**:

eas**y**　　　eas**ier** (than)　　　the eas**iest**
(also: happy, funny, lucky)

Irregular comparatives and superlatives

| good | better (than) | the best |
| bad | worse (than) | the worst |

To talk about two things which are the same, put **as** before the adjective and **as** before the noun:
Venice is **as** *beautiful* **as** *Florence.*

8 Use the prompts to write sentences that are true for you.

English/Maths/difficult
Italian food/English food/good

1 Maths is more difficult than English.....................

4 ....

Geography/Science/easy

5 .... is the best football team in the world.

2 ....

6 .... is the worst singer in the world.

winter/summer/nice

7 .... is the most popular band in my class.

3 ....

8 .... is the nicest person in the world.

9a Complete the questions about your country with the comparative or superlative forms of the adjectives in brackets.

Your country in focus

$7

(popular) **1** Is basketball .more popular than.... football in your country?

(good) **2** Which is ....the best....... football team?

(famous) **3** Who is .... sportsperson?

(interesting) **4** Which is .... place to visit?

(beautiful) **5** Which region of your country is ...., the north or the south?

(high) **6** Which are .... mountains?

(typical) **7** Which are .... dishes in your country?

(difficult) **8** Is your language .... English?

9b Complete the questions about the capital of your country using *as ... as*.

(big) **9** Is the capital of your country **as big as** London?

(old) **10** Is it .... Sydney?

(modern) **11** Is it .... Brasilia?

(expensive) **12** Is it .... New York?

Brasilia

- The population of London is approximately 7.3 million.
- The city of Sydney, Australia, dates from 1788.
- Brasilia, the capital of Brazil, dates from 1956.

Extra!

10 Work with a partner. Ask and answer the questions in Exercise 9. Then write your partner's answers.

A Is basketball more popular than football?

B No, it isn't. Football is more popular.

A Yes, I think so too. / I don't think so. I think basketball is more popular.

Anna thinks that football is more popular than basketball.

11 Write a paragraph about your town. Include:

- the most interesting place to visit
- the best place to spend Saturday afternoon
- places to eat – compare them (better than/more expensive than)
- the most popular shopping street
- the most famous building

My town is called .... The most interesting place to visit is the church. It's near the ....

5

12 **Listen and read.**

Ashan How's the pizza?

Sophie It's OK. But it isn't hot enough.

Ashan I'll put it back in the microwave.

Here you are.

Sophie Ahh! It's too hot now! I can't eat it.

Ashan Oh, you're too fussy. Here, give it to me. I'll eat it.

Grammar focus

too ..., not ... enough

It's too hot.
It isn't hot enough.

Notice the order of the words:
too hot   **not** hot **enough**

Comprehension

13 **Write the names.**

1 ......Ashan....... cooks a pizza for ....

2 .... doesn't like the pizza.

3 .... puts the pizza back in the microwave.

4 .... doesn't eat the pizza.

5 So .... eats it.

Grammar practice

14 **Use the prompts to write sentences with *too* or *not ... enough*.**

1 Sorry, you can't come in. (you/late)
You're too late..............................

2 We mustn't swim here. (It/dangerous)
....

3 You can't all get into the car. (It/big)
....

4 I can't wear these trainers any more. (They/small)
....

5 I'm not good at basketball. (I/tall)
....

62

Write

15 Write sentences with *too* or *not ... enough*.

1 old
You ..*aren't old enough.*..........................

2 big
It ....

3 expensive
They ....

4 long
They ....

5 hot
It ....

6 cold
It ....

🎧 Pronunciation

Final consonants /g/ and /d/

16a **Listen and repeat.**

/g/		/d/	
1	big	4	old
2	dog	5	hard
3	leg	6	cold

16b **Work with a partner. Choose one word from each pair and say it. Your partner must point to the word.**

1	big	bigger
2	old	older
3	cold	colder
4	hard	harder

🎧 Talk time

17a **Choose the correct response.**

I know.	I don't know.
Hang on a minute!	I don't think so.
~~I think so, too.~~	

1 I think Monday's the worst day of the week.
...*I think so, too.*....

2 Which is the highest mountain in Europe?

3 Hurry up! We're going now.

4 I think Michael Owen is the best footballer in the world.

5 We've got an English test on Monday.

17b **Listen and check.**

1 Read the text and complete the biography on page 65.

SPORT NEWS

A Formula One Superstar

Jenson Button is the most famous young British racing driver. But people say that Lewis Hamilton is going to be the new British Motor Racing champion.

Lewis is only 15. So he's five years younger than Jenson Button. Lewis is also too young to have a driving licence. But the Formula 1 team McLaren is paying for him to train and race karts.

Lewis Hamilton lives in Stevenage, a town in Hertfordshire, just north of London. He competes in karting races in Britain and in Europe. He also does karate, goes running and does fitness training.

Next month he's competing in the British Junior Yamaha championship. We wish him the best of luck!

Biography

Name: ...Lewis Hamilton....................................

Age: ....

Home town: ....

Main sport: ....

Other sports: ....

Next competition: ....

Lewis Hamilton Official Website

HOME PAGE

BIOGRAPHY

PHOTOS

STATISTICS

CHAT ROOM

PROFILE

Listen

2 **Listen and complete the rest of the chart.**

Likes and dislikes

Interests		
☐ drums	✓ guitar	
☐ football	☐ basketball	
☐ listening to music	☐ going to the cinema	
☐ partying	☐ reading	
Favourite food ☐ Italian	☐ English	
Favourite football team ☐ Manchester United	☐ Arsenal	
Favourite album ☐ 2PAC's Greatest Hits	☐ The Best of Britney	

Speak

3 **Work with a partner. Ask and answer questions about Lewis and Jenson.**

B: Use the information in the newspaper article in Exercise 1 to answer A's questions.

A's questions	B's answers
1 Is Lewis older or younger than Jenson Button?	Lewis is ....
2 Who is more famous at the moment?	At the moment ....
3 Why hasn't Lewis got a driving licence?	Because ....
4 Where does he live?	....

A: Use the information in the chart in Exercise 2 to answer B's questions.

B's questions	A's answers
1 What does Lewis like doing in his free time?	He likes playing the guitar, ...
2 What does he think about Italian food?	He thinks it's .... than ....
3 Has he got a favourite football team?	Yes, he has. He thinks Arsenal ....
4 What's his favourite album?	It's ....

Write

4 **Continue the newspaper article about Lewis Hamilton. Write about his interests, favourite food, favourite football team and favourite album.**

In his free time, Lewis likes...................................

Let's check

Vocabulary check

1 **Complete each sentence with the correct word from the list.**

> desert   ~~islands~~   lake   mountain range   North
> river   sea   South   volcano   waterfall   west

Corsica, Sicily, Cyprus and Malta are .....islands....... .

1   The Sahara is a ....
2   Etna is a ....
3   The Amazon is a ....
4   The Mediterranean is a ....
5   The Alps are a ....
6   Niagara Falls is a ....
7   Baykal is a .... in Russia.
8   Canada is in .... America.
9   Brazil is in .... America.
10 Ireland is off the .... coast of Britain.

Write your score: .... /10

Grammar check

2 **Complete each sentence with the correct adjective in the comparative or superlative form.**

> easy   ~~famous~~   lucky
> expensive   good   popular

Britney Spears is the .most famous. singer in the world. Everybody knows her.

1   Amy is .... girl in the school. Everybody likes her.
2   Your trainers were .... than mine. Mine were £30 and yours were £40.
3   My brother is .... person in my family. He always wins at cards.
4   I think Ronaldo is .... football player in the world. He's brilliant.
5   Is the Science homework .... this week? Last week it was impossible!

Write your score: .... /5

3 **Complete the sentences with too or n't … enough and an adjective from the box.**

> cold   difficult   expensive   ~~hot~~   long   old

It's .too hot.... in here. Can I open the window?

1   We didn't enjoy swimming yesterday. The water was ....
2   We can't go to the concert. The tickets are .... They're £80.
3   These jeans are .... Can I have a bigger size, please?

4   I can't do the Maths homework. It's .... Can you help me with it?
5   I'm sorry but you can't see that film. You aren't fifteen, so you are ....

Write your score: .... /5

4 **Choose the correct words for each sentence.**

Norway is colder than Egypt.
A cold   **B** too cold   **C** colder

1   These shoes are .... . I'm size 39 and they're size 38.
    A smallest   **B** too small   **C** small
2   My father is … singer in my family.
    A the worse   **B** bad   **C** the worst
3   Which language is …, French or English?
    A easy   **B** easier   **C** easiest
4   Basketball isn't … as football in Spain.
    A as popular   **B** more popular   **C** very popular
5   We can't swim in the lake. The water isn't .... .
    A warmer   **B** too warm   **C** warm enough

Write your score: .... /5

5 **Correct the mistake in each sentence.**

/\ = there's a word missing; X = change one word; ↪ = change the order of two words; * = you must delete one word.

Love is the more important than money. *
Love is more important than money.

1   Carnival is most exciting time of the year in Brazil. /\
    ....
2   I think Enrique Iglesias is most popular than Ricky Martin. X
    ....
3   The Atacama Desert is not big as the Sahara Desert. /\
    ....
4   You can't go camping on your own – you're too younger. X
    ....
5   I can't drive a car yet – I'm not enough old. ↪
    ....

Write your score: .... /5
Write your total score: .... /30

Television programmes

1 **Listen and read.** 🎧

a

(the news)

b
(the weather)

c

(a comedy programme)

d
(a cartoon)

e

(a film)

f
(a sports programme)

g
(a soap opera)

h
(a documentary)

i

(a nature programme)

j

(a quiz show)

k

(a music programme)

l

(the adverts)

2 **Listen. What kind of programmes do they talk about?** 🎧

3 **Now tell your partner about the programmes you like and don't like.**

> **A** What kind of programmes do you like?

> **B** I like comedy programmes, quiz shows and music programmes like *Top of the Pops.*

4 **Write about the programmes you like.**

I like watching cartoons ...

....
....
....
....
....
....
....

Where were you last night?

- Past simple of *be*
- Past simple of regular verbs
- Past time adverbials: *last Saturday, the day before yesterday, yesterday morning/lunchtime/evening*
- Talk about the past

Friday evening ...

Is Sophie there, please?

No, sorry, Alex. She isn't in.

Can I speak to Ashan, please?

No, sorry, Alex. He isn't in.

No, she isn't.

Is Kate in?

Listen and read

1 **Answer the questions.**

1 Who's in the first photo?
2 What's he doing?
3 Who does he call?
4 What's the problem?

Listen and read

2 **Listen and read.**

Saturday morning ...

Alex	Where were you last night, Kate?
Kate	I was with Megan. We were at Guides.
Alex	Where were you, Ashan? Were you at Sophie's house?
Ashan	No, I wasn't. I was at my piano lesson.
Alex	And you weren't at home, Sophie.
Sophie	I was in all evening ... Oh, I was out for about ten minutes at the video shop. Were you at home?
Alex	Yes, I was. You were all out and I was in all evening and there was nothing on TV. I was really bored!
Kate	Ah, never mind! Anyway, *High School from Hell* is on tonight.
Ashan	What's that?
Sophie	It's a new comedy. It's about a school like ours.
Kate	You can all come round and watch it.
Alex	Sounds great!

Comprehension

3a **Where were they? Match the names to the pictures.**

1 Kate ....a............   3 Sophie ....
2 Ashan ....   4 Alex ....

 a   b

 c   d

Answer the questions.

3b
1 What's the new comedy on TV called?
2 When is it on?
3 What's it about?
4 Who's going to watch it?

Grammar focus

Past simple of the verb *be*

Affirmative	Negative
I was (at Guides).	I wasn't (at home).
You were	You weren't
He/She/It was	He/She/It wasn't
We were	We weren't
You were	You weren't
They were	They weren't

Read the dialogue again. Underline examples of the Past simple of *be* in the affirmative and negative.

Grammar practice

4 **Complete the sentences with *was, wasn't, were* or *weren't*.**

1 There ......<u>was</u>.......... nothing on TV last night. We
.... really bored.

2 It's warm today but it .... cold yesterday.

3 I .... at Sophie's house because Mum and
Dad .... out for the evening.

4 We .... in the sea for ages. It .... lovely!
It .... cold at all.

5 You .... very good in the school play.
Well done!

6 Ben and Tom .... at school yesterday
because they .... ill.

Grammar focus

Past simple of the verb *be*

Short answers

Questions	Affirmative	Negative
Was I (at home)?	Yes, I was.	No, I wasn't.
Were you...?	Yes, you were.	No, you weren't.
Was he/she/it...?	Yes, he/she/it was.	No, he/she/it wasn't.
Were we...?	Yes, we were.	No, we weren't.
Were you...?	Yes, you were.	No, you weren't.
Were they...?	Yes, they were.	No, they weren't.

Read the dialogue on page 68 again. Underline
examples of questions and short answers in the Past
simple of *be*.

5 **Complete the sentences.**

1 Where ..<u>were</u>... you last night?

2 Where .... your brother on Saturday?

3 What .... our English homework? Can you
remember?

4 '........... you and Nicola at the cinema yesterday?'
'Yes, we ....'

5 '............ the James Bond film on TV last night?'
'No, it ....'

6 '............. Sophie and Kate at Ashan's house?'
'No, they ....'

7 '................ Kate at Guides last night?'
'Yes, she ....'

8 '................ it nice in Sardinia?' 'Yes, it ....'

Read and speak

6a **Solve the puzzle.**

Puzzle corner

Susie was at home.
One person was at the swimming pool.
Fiona was at the cinema with one of the boys.
Chris and Matt weren't in the same place.
Chris wasn't at the cinema.

Where was he?

	🏠	🏊	🎦
Susie	✓		
Fiona			
Chris			
Matt			

6b **Work with a partner. Ask and answer about Susie, Fiona, Chris and Matt.**

A Where was Susie?

B She was at home. Were Chris and Matt at the swimming pool?

7 Speak and write

**Work with a partner. Ask and answer.
Write your partner's answers.**

Where were you ...
- last Friday evening?
- the day before yesterday?
- yesterday lunchtime?
- yesterday evening?

I was	at	the beach
	in	home
	with	town
		a friend's house
		friends
		the cinema
		school
		my mum and dad
		the park

6

🎧 Listen and read

8 **Listen and read.**

New ▼ | Send | Receive | Forward | Delete

Hi Amy!

How are you? I'm exhausted! I walked 25 kilometres at the weekend with my friend Sophie. It was a sponsored walk to raise money for our local hospital. We started at 7.30 in the morning. It was too early for me. I wasn't awake. We only stopped for about ten minutes for lunch. We finished at 4 o'clock.

When we finished, I called Mum to come and pick us up. She cooked us a huge meal. Then we watched a quiz show on TV. Sophie stayed over. We were in bed by 8 o'clock. The walk was really hard but I collected £100.

Write to me soon.
Love Kate
PS Here are some photos of the walk. You can see I enjoyed it!

55-77-000

b
TOWN HALL BRANCH, SMITHFIELD

One hundred pounds   £100.00

"000177" 547"25: 16233354"

Comprehension

9 Find a sentence in the e-mail for each photo. Then put the photos in the correct order.

Photo a: When we finished, I called Mum to come and pick us up.

70

Grammar focus

Past simple of regular verbs

Affirmative

I walked.	We walked.
You walked.	You walked.
He/She/It walked.	They walked.

To make the Past simple of regular verbs, add **ed**:

walk	walk**ed**
start	start**ed**

If the verb ends in e, just add:

like	like**d**
dance	dance**d**

Grammar practice

10 **Complete the sentences with the Present simple or the Past simple.**

walk

1 He .....walks........ to school every day.

He ....walked...... to school yesterday.

watch

2 I .... *Friends* last night.

I always .... *Friends* on Thursday.

play

3 They usually .... basketball on Saturday.

They .... last Saturday afternoon.

help

4 She .... in the house yesterday.

She sometimes .... in the house when her mum's very busy.

skate

5 We .... to school this morning.

We usually .... when it isn't raining.

enjoy

6 You .... Disney cartoons when you were younger.

You .... *The Simpsons* now.

Read and listen

11a **Read Kate's account of the walk in Exercise 8 and complete the chart for her.**

		Kate	Sophie
1	distance of walk	25 km	20 km
2	start time		
3	lunch break		
4	finish time		
5	evening activity		
6	bedtime		

11b **Now listen to Sophie talking about the walk. There are six differences between her account and Kate's. Complete the chart for Sophie.**

12 **Complete Sophie's e-mail about the walk.**

> From:
> To: @Emily
> Subject:
> Attachments: *none*
>
> Hi Emily!
> How are you? Guess what? I walked 20 kilometres on Saturday. ....
> ....

Speak

13a **Work in pairs. Think about yesterday at school and complete the chart.**

start time:	
break:	
finish time:	
after school: (TV/sport)	

13b **Now tell your partner about your day using the verbs in the box.**

start	stop for a break	finish	watch/play

> I started school at 8 o'clock.

Grammar focus

Past simple of regular verbs

Negative

I/You/He/She/It/We/You/They didn't watch TV.

Questions

Did I/you/he/she/it/we/you/they watch TV?

Short answers

Affirmative

Yes, I/you/he/she/it/we/you/they did.

Negative

No, I/you/he/she/it/we/you/they didn't.

To make negatives in the past tense, put *didn't* between the subject and the verb:

I **didn't** watch the news.

He **didn't** enjoy the film.

To make questions in the past tense, start with *Did:*

Did you phone Kate? **Did** she cycle to school?

For short answers, use *did* and *didn't:*

Yes, I **did. No,** she **didn't.**

Remember, with **did** and **didn't** you use the infinitive of the verb, not the Past simple.

🎧 Listen and read

(14) **Listen and read.**

Alex	Did you watch *Mission Impossible* on TV?
Ashan	No, I didn't watch TV last night.
Alex	What did you do? Did you go out?
Ashan	No, I didn't. I finished my project on rivers for Geography homework and I practised the piano.
Alex	Oh, I just relaxed!

Comprehension

(15) **Answer the questions.**

1 Which film was on TV? <u>Mission Impossible</u>
2 When was the film on?
3 What was Ashan's homework for Geography?
4 What musical instrument does Ashan play?

Grammar practice

(16a) **Use the prompts to write negative sentences in the Past simple.**

1 She finished her homework.
   I / ✗ <u>I didn't finish my homework.</u>
2 We stayed up late.
   They / ✗ ....
3 I enjoyed the match.
   You / ✗ ....
4 He laughed at the cartoon.
   She / ✗ ....
5 They wanted to go out.
   We / ✗ ....

16b **Use the prompts to write questions and short answers in the Past simple.**

1 I played football yesterday.
   you / ? Did you play football yesterday?
   I / ✓ Yes, I did.
   I / ✗ No, I didn't.

2 I liked the film.
   they / ? ....
   they / ✓ ....

3 We collected World Cup football stickers.
   you / ? ....
   we / ✗ ....

4 He played basketball at the weekend.
   she / ? ....
   she / ✓ ....

Listen

17 **Listen and identify the type of programme.**

a) the news
b) the weather
c) a comedy programme
d) a cartoon
e) a film
f) a sports programme
g) a soap opera
h) a documentary
i) a nature programme
j) a quiz show
k) a music programme
l) the adverts

1 ..i..........................   4 ....
2 ....   5 ....
3 ....

Speak

18a **Work with a partner. Write the names of two programmes you watched and two programmes you didn't watch at the weekend.**

✓   ✗
The Simpsons   Top of the Pops

Now tell your partner what you watched and what you didn't watch.

A I watched The Simpsons. I didn't watch
   Top of the Pops or ....

18b **Ask your partner about other programmes. Write his/her answers.**

A Did you watch any sports programmes
   at the weekend?

Write

19 **Write what you and your partner watched and didn't watch at the weekend.**

I watched a film and I watched The Simpsons.
I didn't watch .... Alexandra watched .... We both
watched ....

Pronunciation
/t/ /d/ /ɪd/

20a **Listen and repeat. Notice the three different sounds at the end of the words.**

/t/	/d/	/ɪd/
walked	called	started
stopped	stayed	skated
....	....	....
....	....	....
....	....	....
....	....	....

20b **Now listen to these words and write them in the correct column.**

Talk time

21a **Choose the correct responses.**

1 Are you doing anything this evening?   ......d......
2 When is High School from Hell on?   ....
3 We'll have a barbecue tonight.   ....
4 What's the film about?   ....
5 Will you be out for long?   ....

a Only for about ten minutes.
b It's about a dog and a wizard.
c Sounds great!
d ~~No, you can come round.~~
e It's on tonight.

21b **Now listen and check.**

Extra!

22 **Practise the dialogues with a partner. Change some of the words if you can.**

A Are you doing anything this weekend?

B No. We can go out.

Star Wars

Read and write

1) **Read about Natalie Portman. Then find similar information about Hayden Christensen.**

1 Natalie Portman is from the United States.	1 Hayden Christensen is from Canada.
2 She's American.	2
3 Natalie Portman first starred in a film at the age of 12.	3
4 She was in a pizza restaurant in New York when an agent noticed her.	4
5 She was 15 when she started work on her first *Star Wars* film *Episode I: The Phantom Menace*.	5
6 Natalie played Queen Padme Amidala.	6
7 After High School, Natalie was a student for 3 years at Harvard University in the United States.	7
8 In her free time, Natalie likes writing, dancing and spending time with her friends.	8

Biography Hayden Christensen

Date of birth

April 19, 1981

Place of birth

Vancouver, Canada

Nationality

Canadian

First film/TV appearance

In an advertisement for crisps when he was 10 years old.

How did he start?

An agent noticed him. His older sister was at an audition and he was with her, because there was nobody at home to look after him!

First Star Wars film

Episode II: Attack of the Clones, aged 19

Star Wars character

Anakin Skywalker

Education

High School in Toronto
The Lee Strasberg Theatre Institute, New York

Interests

He plays tennis and ice hockey and he goes roller-blading.

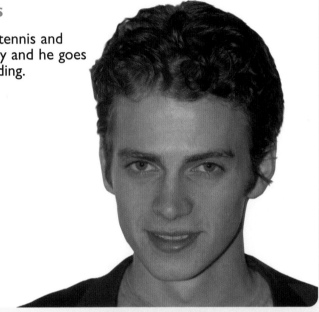

 Listen

2 **Listen to the interviews. Did Kelly and Tara like the new *Star Wars* film? Tick (✓) the chart according to their opinions.**

	Kelly	Tara	Your partner
The special effects were brilliant.	✓		
The special effects weren't very good.			
The actors were excellent.			
The actors weren't very good.			
The film was too long.			
The film wasn't long enough.			
It was better than Episode II.			
It wasn't as good as Episode II.			

Speak

3 **Work with a partner. Ask and answer the questions about a film. Tick (✓) the chart to record your partner's opinions.**

1 Did you like the special effects in the new (*Star Wars/Spiderman/James Bond*) film?
2 What were the actors like?
3 Was the film too long?
4 Was it better than the last (*Star Wars/Spiderman/James Bond*) film?

Portfolio

4 **Write a review for your school magazine describing an interesting film or TV programme. Go to page 130.**

Culture spot
Guides and Scouts

Read

1 Read about Guides and Scouts.

Girlguiding UK is part of an international organisation with 10 million members in the world. Girls go to **Guides** to make friends, to play sports and to learn practical skills. The Girl Guides Association started in 1910.

Last month we camped in tents near a river. We learned how to use a map and a compass and we followed a treasure trail. We cooked all our own meals. And we stayed up all night and talked. It was great!

In the summer we're going to the first ever Girlguiding Football Festival Weekend. We'll play matches against other Guide teams and we'll have coaching from professional players. On Saturday night there will be a karaoke disco. That'll be fun!

Brownies are younger Guides, aged between 7 and 10. They meet every week, play games and have fun. They wear a yellow and brown uniform. More than one in three 8-year-olds in the UK is a Brownie.

When I was seven, I joined the Brownies. We learned team games and worked for our badges.

Cubs are for boys aged 7 to 10. When they're 11, boys can join the **Scouts**. The Boy Scout Association started in 1908.

I was in the Cubs when I was eight. We worked for our badges. We cleaned cars and helped people. There was Cub Camp every summer which was fun. After Cubs I didn't join the Scouts because I was too busy with other activities and sports.

Comprehension

2 **Answer the questions.**

1 Which is older, the Girl Guides Association or the Boy Scout Association?

The Boy Scout Association.

| Cubs | Guides | Scouts | Brownies |

2 Which clubs are for girls and which are for boys?

....

....

3 Which clubs are for younger children?

....

4 What did Kate do last month with the Guides?

....

5 What's she going to do in the summer?

....

....

6 What sort of jobs did Alex do in the Cubs?

....

7 Was he in the Scouts?

....

Vocabulary

3 **Find words in the text for these pictures:**

1 treasure trail

3 ....

4 ....

2 ....

5 ....

Write

4 **Which clubs or groups are there in your country for:**

7- to 10-year-olds?

....

11- to 16-year-olds?

....

Write two paragraphs.

In my country, 7- to 10-year-olds can ....

6 Let's check

Vocabulary check

1 **Read the words heard on TV and write the type of programme next to them.**

advert	news
documentary	quiz show
cartoon	soap opera
~~comedy programme~~	sports programme
music programme	weather
nature programme	

The Arnold family and their crazy kids are in trouble again. Get ready to laugh!

<u>comedy programme</u>...

1 And it's a goal for Real Madrid!

....

2 Eek! It's that craaaaaaaazy cat again!!!!

....

3 The President is flying to Washington today.

....

4 These birds go to Africa in the winter.

....

5 This week Britney Spears goes up to number one.

....

6 Tomorrow it will be cold and cloudy in New York.

....

7 Use BLONDIE. It's the best shampoo for blondes.

....

8 You have 20 seconds to answer the next question.

....

9 I really like you, Kylie. I want you to stay with me.

....

10 Horses are very important to the people of Mongolia.

....

Write your score ..../10

Grammar check

2 **Complete the dialogue with the Past simple of the verb in brackets.**

A I <u>called</u>.... (call) you last night but you
(**1**) .... (not/answer) the phone.
(**2**) .... (you/be) out?

B No, I (**3**) .... (not/be). There (**4**) .... (be) a brilliant nature programme on TV about African animals.

A I know. I (**5**) .... (watch) it, too.

B (**6**)............................. (you/like) it?

A Yes. I really (**7**) .... (like) the giraffes. They (**8**) .... (be) so beautiful.

B Anyway, why (**9**) .... (you/call) me last night?

A To tell you about the TV programme.
I (**10**) .... (want) you to watch it, too!

Write your score: .... /10

3 **Choose the correct words for each sentence.**

I **was**. late for school yesterday.
A am   **B** was   **C** were

1 "Did you see Jade last night?" "Yes, I ...."
A saw   **B** see   **C** did

2 "Were Dan and Luke in the park?" "No, they ...."
A wasn't   **B** weren't   **C** didn't

3 Emma and Alex .... Sara's party on Saturday.
A enjoy   **B** like   **C** enjoyed

4 Joey .... in the match last week.
A didn't play   **B** play   **C** plays

5 .... angry about the mess?
A Did they   **B** Were they   **C** Was they

6 "Did he give you the message?" "No, he .... "
A don't   **B** didn't   **C** doesn't

7 What .... at the cinema?
A did you see   **B** you saw   **C** you did see

8 .... any new people at the tennis club?
A Was it   **B** Were they   **C** Were there

9 .... a good time at the beach?
A Did they   **B** Were they   **C** Did they have

10 .... you at the hospital yesterday?
A Did   **B** Visited   **C** Were

Write your score ..../10

4 **Correct the mistake in each sentence.**
/\ = there's a word missing; X = change one word; ⤷ = change the order of two words; * = you must delete one word.

You did watch the match on TV yesterday? ⤷
<u>Did you watch the match on TV yesterday.</u>

1 How many people there at Julie's party yesterday? /\

....

....

2 Did you enjoyed the pancakes this morning? X

....

....

3 We walked 25 kilometres on last weekend.*

....

....

4 You all play very well in the match yesterday. X

....

....

5 Where she was at five o'clock? ⤷

....

....

Write your score: .... /5
Write your total score: .... /35

How good are you?

★ I'm not very good at this. ★★ I'm OK at this. ★★★ I'm good at this.

Tick (✓) the correct boxes.

	★	★★	★★★
READING I can understand:			
a quiz comparing geographical features — *Is the USA bigger than Canada? Which is the biggest country in the world?*			
a magazine article comparing sports stars — *He's five years younger than Jenson Button.*			
an e-mail about last weekend's activities — *I walked 25 kilometres at the weekend.*			
biographical data — *Date of birth: April 19, 1981.*			
a text about Guides and Scouts — *When they're 11, boys can join the Scouts.*			
LISTENING I can understand:			
a conversation about a sports star — *He likes listening to music.*			
an e-mail about last weekend's activities — *Kate's mum picked us up. We were really hungry.*			
different types of TV programmes — *... a beautiful goal for this talented young striker ...*			
people giving their opinions about a film — *I liked the special effects.*			
WRITING I can write:			
sentences comparing two things — *Geography is easier than Science.*			
about my favourite and least favourite people and things — *... is the nicest person in the world/... is the worst singer in the world.*			
about places to visit in my town — *The best place to eat is ....*			
information to complete a simple form — *Name: Lewis Hamilton, Age: 15*			
sentences based on information in an article — *In his free time, Lewis likes playing the guitar.*			
about past experiences — *Last Saturday afternoon I was in town and ...*			
a film or TV review — *Last week, I saw King Arthur. It was wonderful.*			
SPEAKING I can:			
ask and answer questions about sports stars — *Why hasn't Lewis got a driving licence? Because he's too young.*			
ask and answer questions about where people were — *Where were you the day before yesterday? I was at the beach.*			
talk about yesterday at school. — *I started school at 8 o'clock.*			
ask and answer questions about watching TV at the weekend — *I watched The Simpsons. I didn't watch the news. Did you watch the match?*			
ask and answer questions about a film — *Did you like the special effects in the new James Bond film?*			

Vocabulary groups

Write five more words in each vocabulary group.

Geographical features ....river.... ...mountain. ....

Television programmes news cartoon ....

Module 4

Oh, dear!

Grammar

Quantifiers: *a lot of/lots of, plenty of, a few, a little, many, much*

Past simple of irregular verbs

ago

Past simple of regular and irregular verbs

could for requests

R Imperatives, revision

Vocabulary

R Food, revision

Prepositions of motion

Communication

Talking about past events

Making and responding to requests

Asking for and giving directions

Pronunciation

/eɪ/ and /e/

/ə/

Culture spot

Famous kings and queens

7

Food

1a Match the words to the pictures.

apple	cheese	milk
banana	chicken	salad
bread	coffee	tea
butter	egg	tomato
cereal	ham	

1b Listen and check. 🎧

2 Listen and read. 🎧

1 .... bread ....

2  ....

3 ....

4  ....

5 ....

6 ....

7 ....

8  ....

9  ....

10 ....

11 ....

12 ....

13 ....

14 ....

Fruit

orange

grapes

lemon

melon

Meat

beef

lamb

Fish

sardines

salmon

Vegetables

onions

carrots

beans

potatoes

mushrooms

peas

rice

flour

sugar

oil

salt

pepper

vinegar

We made lots of pancakes!

- **Quantifiers:** *a lot of/lots of, plenty of, many, much, a few, a little*
- **Past simple of irregular verbs**
- **Talking about past events**

🎧 Listen and read

1 **Listen and read.**

It's Shrove Tuesday – Pancake Day

Ashan	What do we need for the pancakes?
Kate	Eggs, flour and milk.
Ashan	There aren't many eggs in the fridge.
Kate	How many are there?
Ashan	Six.
Kate	That's plenty. Is there much milk left?
Ashan	Yes, there's lots of milk.
Jamie	And there's plenty of flour … Oops! Oh, dear!
Kate	There was plenty of flour. We need a few lemons.
Jamie	Ugh! What for?
Kate	Well, you put lemon juice on the pancakes. And some sugar.
Jamie	I want lots of sugar and just a little lemon juice on mine.

Comprehension

2 **Put the photos on page 83 in the correct order.**

1 ......f........

Do you remember when to use **some** and **any**? Write them in the correct places in the chart.

Grammar focus

Quantifiers: *a lot of/lots of, plenty of, a few, a little, many, much*

	Affirmative	Negative	Questions
Plural countable nouns pancakes, lemons, eggs	a lot of/lots of plenty of, a few	many	plenty of, many
Uncountable nouns milk, sugar, lemon juice	a lot of/lots of plenty of, a little	much	plenty of, much
	We've got a lot of milk. We've got plenty of flour. We've only got a few eggs. Add a little lemon juice.	We haven't got many lemons. There isn't much milk.	Have we got many eggs? Is there much milk left?

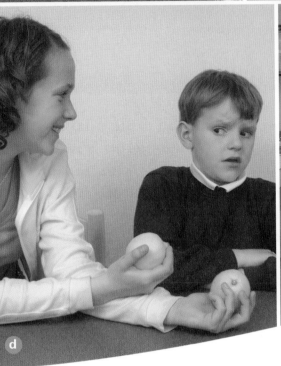

Grammar practice

3 **Complete the sentences with the correct word or words.**

1 There isn't (much/many) .....much........ milk in the bottle.

2 We haven't got (plenty of/many) ....
sweets left.

3 I haven't got (much/many) .... money.

4 There weren't (much/many) .... people at the party.

5 Do you drink (much/many) .... water during the day?

6 It's OK. Don't hurry. We've got (lots of/much) .... time.

7 There are (a few/a little) .... apples in the fridge.

8 Can I have (a few/a little) .... sugar on my cereal?

Write

4a **Write sentences about yourself using the phrases in the chart.**

I've got/I haven't got	a lot of/lots of
I play/I don't play	plenty of
I watch/I don't watch	a few
I eat/I don't eat	many
I drink/I don't drink	much
	any

1 friends .... I've got lots of friends...........

2 good friends ....

3 money..

4 cousins ....

5 aunts and uncles..

6 CDs..

7 sports ....

8 cartoons/documentaries ....

9 fruit/meat/salad/cheese...............................

10 milk/water/fruit juice ....

4b **Tell the class about yourself using the sentences you've written.**

Listen and read

5 **Listen and read.**

On Pancake Day we went to my aunt's house and we made lots of pancakes. Then we ate them with sugar and lemon juice. We had a great time.

Sophie

It was my birthday last Friday. I had a brilliant day. My friends gave me presents and cards at school. Then, in the evening, my mum and dad took us to the cinema. We saw a really good film and afterwards we came home and Dad made us a really nice meal.

Alex

Comprehension

6 **Match the pictures to the people.**

Sophie ...c... **Alex**

a presents

b cinema

c sugar & lemon

d pancakes

e chicken dinner

Hello, Sophie!

f people at door

Listen and write

7 **Work with a partner. Listen and write Alex's birthday menu.**

Grammar focus

Past simple of the irregular verb *go*
Affirmative
I/You/He/She/It/We/You/They **went** to the cinema.

Lots of verbs have an irregular past simple in English. Just learn a few at a time.

Grammar practice

8a Make a chart like this in your notebook.

Irregular Past simple verbs

Infinitive	Past simple
go	went
make	made

8b Match the infinitive of each verb to the Past simple and write them in your chart.

Infinitive

go   make   eat   have   give   see   come   take

Past simple

came   made   gave   ate   took   went   had   saw

9 Complete the sentences with the verbs from Exercise 8b in the Past simple.

1 My mum ....**made**........ me a cake for my birthday.
2 We .... swimming yesterday evening.
3 My cousins .... a barbecue last Saturday afternoon.
4 I .... a really good film on TV last night.
5 The dog .... my dinner.
6 She .... me a CD for my birthday.
7 My Canadian uncle .... to see us last week.
8 My grandparents .... me to the cinema last Friday.

/eɪ/ and /e/

10a Listen and repeat.

/eɪ/	/e/
day	egg
great	lemon

10b Listen and write the words in the correct column.

1 play	4 head
2 plenty	5 came
3 made	6 then

/eɪ/	/e/
day	egg
great	lemon
....	....
....	....
....	....

Write and speak

11a Write about your birthday or another special day. Use the words from the chart to help you.

I had a brilliant day on my birthday. I ....

I	had	a brilliant day
My friends	went	a birthday cake
My mum/dad/	came	lots of presents
brother/sister		some cards
We		a party

	gave		to the cinema
	made	(me)	to a restaurant
	took		to the beach
			to the mountains
			to my house

11b Tell your partner about your special day.

I had a brilliant birthday.

Read

12 Look at the photos and put the dialogue in the correct order.

..........1b..........

a **Sophie** Oh no, what did he do?
Kate He said, 'You did that on purpose!' Then he took the pancake and threw it at me.

c **Kate** Then I tossed a pancake and ...

e **Ashan** ... it fell on Jamie's head. He wasn't happy!

b **Kate** Did you make pancakes at home last night?
Sophie No, we didn't. We went out.
Kate Oh, we made lots of pancakes.
Ashan And we got into a lot of trouble.

d **Sophie** Why?
Kate Well, first Jamie dropped the flour and it went all over the floor.

f **Ashan** And it didn't hit Kate.
Kate Just then, my dad came into the kitchen and it hit him on the head.

Listen

13 **Listen and check.**

Grammar focus

Past simple of irregular verbs

Negative

I/You/He/She/It/We/You/They   didn't (go).

Questions

Did   I/you/he/she/it/we/you/they   (go)?

Short answers

Affirmative	**Negative**
Yes, I did.	No, I didn't.

 You make negatives, questions and short answers with *did* and *didn't*, just as you do for regular verbs.

Grammar practice

14a **Find the Past simple of these verbs in the dialogue.**

do	fall	get	make	hit	throw

14b **Complete the dialogue using the correct form of the verbs in Exercise 14a. Alex is talking to Kate about Pancake Day.**

Alex	...Did.. you .make. pancakes last night?
Kate	Yes, we .did.... .
Alex	Were they good?
Kate	The first ones weren't very good. And then we .... into trouble with my dad.
Alex	Why, what .... you do?
Kate	Well, I tossed a pancake...
Alex	And it fell on the floor.
Kate	No, it .... fall on the floor. It .... on Jamie's head.
Alex	Did he ....get..... angry?
Kate	Yes, he .... He said, 'You did that on purpose!' Then he .... it at me.
Alex	.... it hit you?
Kate	No, it .... It .... my dad.

14c **Now listen and check.**

Speak

15 **Work with a partner. Ask and answer about last weekend. Use the verbs in the table and any others you can remember.**

played	watched	relaxed	worked	phoned
went	did	had	made	took

A What did you do last weekend?

B I went to the cinema on Saturday evening and my grandparents took me to a football match on Sunday afternoon.

 Talk time

16a **Listen and repeat.**

1 We **got into a lot of trouble.**
2 It went **all over** the floor.
3 You did that **on purpose**!
4 **Just then**, my dad came in.
5 He **wasn't happy**!

16b **Find a phrase to complete the dialogues. Then practise them with a partner.**

A Why did you get into trouble at school today?

B I threw a rubber at Ben and ......*just then*.......... the teacher came into the room.

A We were very late for school.

B Yes, we ....

A I dropped a glass of water.

B Don't tell me. It went .... your homework.

A Did your teacher get angry?

B Well, She ....

A Oops! Sorry!

B You did that ....!

Portfolio

17 **Write an article for your school magazine about a special day. Go to page 131.**

Skills development

Special days ... in Japan

Read

1 **Read the text. Meiko tells us about special days in Japan.**

December 31st – January 1st

At the end of December, we send cards to each other. On December 31st, we go to the temple. The temple bells ring 101 times to welcome the New Year. When we come home, we have a big meal before we go to bed. Then we have another special meal when we get up!

Last year I sent about a hundred cards to my friends. Just before midnight, we went to the temple and when we came home we had a meal. Then in the morning we opened our *jubako* boxes. Inside there were beans, eggs, fish, meat and vegetables. Each food has a special meaning like 'health', 'money', 'a long life' and 'a happy life'. We ate a lot!

February 3rd / 4th

February 3rd or 4th is *Setsubun*. It's the end of winter and the start of spring. People dress up as devils and you throw beans at them to keep bad things away.

> Our teachers dressed up as devils with red and blue faces and we threw beans at them! We really enjoyed it!

March 3rd

> Yesterday my mum and I made our *hina-dan*. It looked beautiful!

March 3rd is Girls' Day. Girls and their mothers make a display called a *hina-dan* in the best room of the house. The *hina-dan* has seven steps and on each step there are dolls. The two at the top are the Emperor and his wife.

Comprehension

(2) **Answer the questions. Be careful! Some questions are in the present tense and some are in the past tense.**

1 Why do the temple bells ring on December 31st?
They ring to welcome the New Year.

2 How many New Year cards did Meiko send to her friends?

3 What was inside the *jubako* box?

4 What does *Setsubun* celebrate?

5 Why do people throw beans at the devils?

6 What did the teachers at Meiko's school do at *Setsubun*?

7 What do girls and their mothers do in Japan on March 3rd?

8 Which dolls go at the top of the *hina-dan*?

9 What happens on Boys' Day in Japan?

10 Whose was the biggest kite? Toshi's or Takuma's?

May 5th

May 5th is Boys' Day. We put kites in the shape of fish in parks and outside the house. There is one fish for each boy in the family. When the wind blows, the fish seem to swim!

My brothers put their kites outside the house this morning. Toshi's was the smallest, because he's the youngest. Takuma's was the biggest, because he's the oldest.

Listen

 Listen

(3a) **Choose the activity for each special day and write it in the chart.**

Special days in Britain	Date	Activity
Christmas Day	December 25th	_We ate turkey and Christmas pudding_
Pancake Day	February/March	....
Valentine's Day	February 14th	....
		....
Easter	March/April	....
		....
Hallowe'en	October 31st	....
		....
Bonfire Night	November 5th	....

We made pancakes.   We ate turkey and Christmas pudding.   My mum and dad gave me a big chocolate egg.

We dressed up as witches and ghosts.   We had fireworks.   I made a card and sent it to my boyfriend.

(3b) **Now listen and check.**

Speak

(4) **Work with a partner. Which is your favourite special day? Ask and answer questions about it.**

> A Where did you go and what did you do?

> B What did you eat?

Write

(5) **Write about your special day.**

My special day is May 1st because on this day we usually ....

Let's check

Vocabulary check

1 **Write the name of the food under each picture.**

__chicken__   1 _____   2 _____

3 _____   4 _____   5 _____

Write your score: ..../5

Grammar check

2 **Choose the correct word for each sentence.**

How ....**many**..... cousins have you got in Australia?
A much   (**B** many)   **C** plenty

1 How .... milk do you want in your coffee?
A much   **B** many   **C** few

2 There weren't .... people at the party.
A much   **B** many   **C** a lot

3 My cat doesn't drink .... water.
A much   **B** many   **C** a lot

4 Let's take .... apples with us.
A a little   **B** a few   **C** a lot

5 We ate .... of sweets yesterday.
A a little   **B** a few   **C** a lot

6 Hurry up. We haven't got .... time.
A much   **B** many   **C** a little

7 Did you play in .... matches last month?
A much   **B** many   **C** lots

8 Let's have a party. We've got .... good CDs.
A much   **B** few   **C** plenty of

9 She's got .... friends.
A lots   **B** plenty   **C** a lot of

10 There's .... lemonade in the bottle.
A a little   **B** a few   **C** a lot

Write your score: ..../10

3 **Complete the questions with *much* or *many*. Put the verbs in the Past simple.**

Q: How ..**many**.... times __did she fall__ (she /fall) off the horse?

A: She (**1**) .... (fall) off three times, poor thing.

1 **Q:** How (**2**) .... pancakes (**3**) .... (you /make) this morning?

A: I (**4**) ....(not make) any.

2 **Q:** How (**5**) .... money (**6**) .... (you / find) on the floor yesterday?

A: I (**7**) .... (find)   10.

3 **Q:** How (**8**) .... cards (**9**) .... (she /get) for her birthday?

A: She (**10**) .... (get) twenty.

Write your total score ...... /10

4 **Correct the mistake in each sentence. /\ = there's a word missing; ✗ = change one word; ↪ = change the order of two words; * = you must delete one word.**

We made a lots of sandwiches for the picnic. *
__We made lots of sandwiches for the picnic...__

1 There are't much eggs left. ✗
....
....

2 There are plenty lemons on the table. /\
....
....

3 How many cards you did get for your birthday? ↪
....
....

4 Can you buy few apples at the market? /\
....
....

5 Did the teacher got angry with you? ✗
....
....

Write your score ...... /5

Write your total score ...... /30

Prepositions of motion

1 **Listen and follow.** 🎧

1 into

2 up

3 down

4 over

5 under

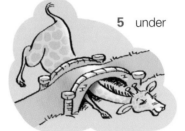

6 across

7 through

8 along

9 past

10 towards

2 **How many sentences can you make?**

Jump into the lake.

go	into	the path
	up	the bridge
run	down	the house
	over	the forest
swim	under	the river
	across	the lake
jump	through	the waterfall
	along	the mountain
	past	the cave
	towards	the desert

8

That was 500 years ago!

- *ago*
- **Past simple of regular and irregular verbs**
- *could* **for requests**
- **Imperatives, revision**
- **Making and responding to requests**
- **Asking for and giving directions**

Listen and read

1 **Listen and read.**

1 Kate's dad is taking Kate, Sophie, Ashan and Alex to Hampton Court Palace.

What time's the next train?

2 **Comprehension**

Put the sentences in the correct order to tell story of the trip to Hampton Court.

.... We found him in the end ... in the café!

.... We bought some postcards and things in the shop.

.... The cycle ride to Hampton Court took about an hour and a half.

.... We got off at Richmond.

.... We had a picnic in the garden when we got there.

.... Alex got lost in the maze.

...1.... We put our bikes on the train at West Hampstead.

.... We went into the palace.

Read

2 They get off at Richmond.

3 **Match the questions to the answers.**

..1 j........

1 Where did they go?

2 How did they get there?

3 How long did it take to travel from Richmond to Hampton Court?

4 What did they do when they got there?

5 What did they do after the picnic?

6 Who lived at Hampton Court Palace?

7 What did they do after they visited the palace?

8 Where did Alex get lost?

9 Did they find him? Where?

10 Did they buy anything?

a Henry VIII.

b Yes, they found him in the end ... in the café!

c They bought some postcards and things in the shop.

d It took about an hour and a half.

e They went by train and then they cycled along the river path.

f They went into the maze.

g They had a picnic in the garden.

h Alex got lost in the maze.

i They went into the palace.

j They went to Hampton Court Palace.

4 **Speak**

Work with a partner. Cover the answers in Exercise 3.

Partner A: Ask Partner B questions 1–5.
Partner B: Ask Partner A questions 6–10.

Grammar focus

ago

That was five hundred years ago.
I saw him a minute ago.
Two years ago, I went to London with my parents.

How do you say these sentences in your language?

Grammar practice

5 **Write how long ago these things were.**

1 The Olympic Games were in Barcelona in 1992.
   <u>That was ... years ago.</u>

2 The World Cup was in Italy in 1990.

3 The Americans landed on the moon in 1969.

4 The first Tour de France cycle race was in 1903.

5 In 1932, Amelia Earhart was the first woman to fly across the Atlantic.

Here are some more irregular verbs to add to your list.

| buy – bought | find – found | put – put |

Extra!

6 **Answer the questions about yourself using *ago*.**

1 When did you last go to a birthday party?

> I went to a birthday party two weeks ago.

2 When did you last eat chocolate ice cream?

3 When did you last go on a train?

4 When did you last buy a present for your mum?

5 When did you last see a really funny film?

6 When did you last have a picnic?

8

🎧 Listen and read

7 **Listen and read.**

Tourist	Excuse me, could you tell me the way to Station Road?
Dad	Yes, of course. It's not far. Go straight on along this path. Turn right when you get to the road. Turn left at the roundabout. That's High Street. Take the third turning on the right. That's Station Road.
Tourist	Thank you.

Comprehension

8 **Match the directions to the pictures.**

1 Go straight on. 2 Turn left.

3 Turn right. 4 Take the first turning on the right.

a   b

c   d

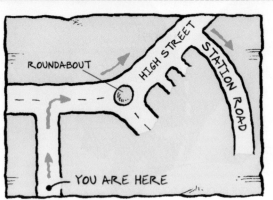

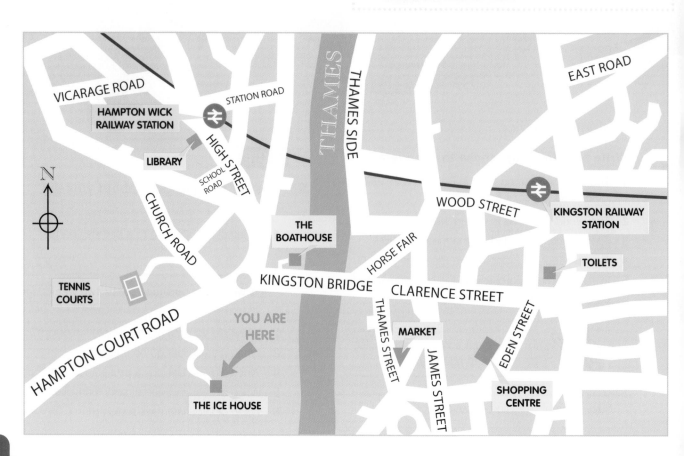

Read

9 **Read the directions and look at the map in Exercise 8. Start from the Ice House. Work out what the destinations are.**

1 It's not far. Go along this path. Turn right when you get to the road. Cross the road and go along Church Road. Take the first turning on the left. It's a path. Go along the path. They're on your left.

2 It's not far. Go along this path. Turn right when you get to the road. At the roundabout turn right but don't go over the bridge to the other side of the river. It's on your left.

3 It's quite a long way. Go along this path. Turn right when you get to the road. At the roundabout turn right. Go over the bridge. Don't go left along Horse Fair. Go straight on along Clarence Street. Take the first on the right. That's Thames Street. It's on your left.

Grammar focus

Could for polite requests

Could you tell me the way to the station?
Yes, of course./No, sorry. I'm afraid I can't.

Could you post this letter for me?

Could we have our ball back, please?

Could I use your phone, please?
Yes, of course./No, sorry. I'm afraid you can't.

Could I borrow your bike?

Could I leave a message?

In each of these sentences it is possible to use **can**, but **could** sounds more polite.

Grammar practice

10 **Work with a partner. Make polite requests using the prompts.**

1 I/borrow

<u>Could I borrow your dictionary?</u>
[✓] <u>Yes, of course.</u>................

2 I/borrow

....
[✗] ....

---

3 I/listen to

....
[✓] ....

4 I/use

....
[✓] ....

5 you/pass me

....
[✓] ....

6 you/carry

....
[✗] ....

Talk time

11a **Listen and repeat.**

1 Excuse me.
2 Could you tell me the way to ...?
3 Is it far?
4 It's quite a long way.
5 It's not far.

11b **Work with a partner. Ask for and give directions to one of the places on the map, starting from the Ice House.**

A Excuse me, could you tell me the way to ...

B Yes, of course. It's not far. Go along this path. Turn ....

11c **Work with a partner. Ask for and give directions.**

A Think of a place of interest, a café or a shop near your school. Imagine you're an English tourist. Ask Partner B for directions.
B Give Partner A directions.

12 Write

Write the directions you gave in Exercise 11c.

<u>Walk along the road, then turn right</u>.......

Treasure Island

Start here

Listen and read

13 **Listen and read. Look at the picture of Treasure Island. Write the letters of the places in the order they are mentioned.**

1 j.(the track)........

Sophie	That's enough homework. Let's play Treasure Island on the computer.
Ashan	Good idea. 'The treasure's in the north-east of the island.' OK, then. Go along the track.
Sophie	No, there are tigers there! I'm going to go across the field.
Ashan	Right. Then go through the forest towards the volcano.
Sophie	Oh, no, there are snakes!
Ashan	Go up the volcano then.
Sophie	The volcano's erupting ...
Ashan	Come down! No, jump into the lake, quick!
Sophie	OK, I'll swim across the lake and under the waterfall.
Ashan	Don't go into the cave. Go past it.
Sophie	Why?
Ashan	Because there's a dragon in there.
Sophie	I think the treasure's in the pyramid.
Ashan	I think so too. Try it.
Both	Yes!

Pronunciation

/ə/

14a **Listen and repeat.**

1 <u>a</u>cross
2 ov<u>er</u>
3 t<u>o</u>wards
4 cent<u>re</u>

14b **Listen and underline the /ə/ sound in each word.**

1 along
2 about
3 river
4 ago
5 tiger

6 treasure
7 under
8 water
9 letter
10 roundabout

Listen and speak

15a **Listen and choose the correct drawing.**

1   a    b

2   a    b

3   a    b

4   a    b

5   a

1 ....b..........   4 ....
2 ....   5 ....
3 ....

15b **Choose a drawing and give your partner the instruction.**

A Go towards the cave.

B 1a

A Yes, that's right.

Extra!

16 **Work with a partner. Choose a place to hide the treasure. Write out the instructions. Then read them to your partner. Your partner has to find the treasure.**

Go across the desert to the east of the island ....

Was this the Roman *Titanic?*

Two thousand years ago a large ship was in the Mediterranean to the south of Italy. It was a ship for very rich Roman families who sailed along the coast of Italy from port to port. There was a big storm and the ship sank.

Who found it?

Last year, Giuseppe Russo went swimming near Ragusa, in Sicily. Suddenly, he saw the face of a black panther under the water. 'I pulled it out and discovered that it was part of an oil lamp,' he said. 'Then I found more treasure in the sand. It was like magic!'

What did he find?

Giuseppe found jewels and statues of Roman gods, like Mercury.

Where was it?

The ship was very near the beach. But it was under the sand for 2,000 years, until a storm came last year.

What was the ship like?

It was about fifty metres long, one of the largest Roman ships ever. It was like a Roman villa. There were beautiful living rooms. There were fires and lights. It even had a large bath – with hot water!

Read

1 **Read the article and number the pictures in the order of the text.**

a

b

`1`

c

d

e

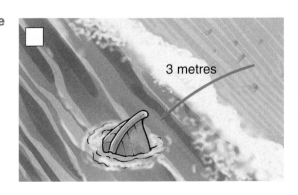

3 metres

Listen

2 **Listen and answer the questions.**

1 Where was the ship exactly?
  It was near the coast of Sicily.......

2 What was Giuseppe Russo's job?

3 How tall was the statue of Mercury?

4 How far was the ship from the beach?

5 What were there in the ship's living rooms?

Speak

3 **Work with a partner. Ask and answer the questions.**

> **A** Where was the ship?

> **B** It was in the Mediterranean, to the south of Italy. It was near the coast of Sicily.

A

Where was the ship?

1 Who sailed on the ship?

2 Why did the ship sink?

3 When did the ship sink?

4 What was the name of the swimming teacher?

5 What did he see under the water?

6 What else did he find in the sand?

B

1 What kind of statue did he find?

2 How tall was it?

3 How long was the ship under the sand?

4 Was it a small ship?

5 How far was the ship from the beach?

6 Was there a swimming pool on the ship?

Write

4 **Imagine you were on holiday last year and you found something interesting. Write an account of what you found.**

Where were you?

What did you find?

Where did you find it?

What did you do with it?

Culture spot

Famous kings and queens

Read

1 **Read about three historical figures.**

Henry VIII

Henry VIII was born on 28th June, 1481. He became King of England at the age of 17. He was tall (1.83 metres), strong and energetic. He liked sports. He wrote poetry and was a good musician. In addition to English, he spoke Italian, Latin and Spanish.

Henry left the Catholic Church because he wanted to divorce his first wife, Catherine of Aragon. He made England a Protestant country.

Elizabeth I

Elizabeth I, Henry VIII's daughter, was born at Greenwich Palace in London on 7th September, 1533, nearly 500 years ago. She was twenty-five when she became queen. She was an elegant, slim woman with red hair and a strong personality. She never married and she had no children.

Elizabeth's reign was a time of great discovery. Sir Walter Raleigh, Sir Francis Drake and Sir John Hawkins all sailed across the Atlantic to the Americas. They brought back exotic new plants and food, like tobacco, coffee, potatoes and chocolate. During Elizabeth's reign the first theatres opened in London and William Shakespeare wrote plays for them.

Elizabeth II

Britain is still a monarchy. The queen, Elizabeth II, is head of state. In 2002 she celebrated her Golden Jubilee, fifty years of her reign. Thousands of people went to London to see the celebrations. There was a pop concert in the gardens of Buckingham Palace and a fantastic firework display.

Some people think that a monarchy is old-fashioned and that a republic is better. So will Elizabeth's grandson, Prince William, ever be king?

Comprehension

2 **Read the article and find:**

1 four languages
2 three discoverers
3 two foods
4 one writer

3 **Answer the questions.**

Henry VIII

1 How old was Henry VIII when he became king?
....

2 What was he like?
....

3 What was he good at?
....

4 Who was his first wife?
....

5 Why did he leave the Catholic Church?

....

Elizabeth I

6 In which year did Elizabeth I become queen?
....

7 What was special about her reign?
....

8 What did Sir Walter Raleigh do?
....

9 Which famous English writer lived in Elizabeth's time?

....

Elizabeth II

10 Is Britain a monarchy or a republic?
....

11 Who is Britain's head of state?

....

12 How many years ago did she celebrate 50 years of her reign?

....

13 Where did she celebrate?

....

14 What kind of celebrations were there?

....

15 Do all British people think that a monarchy is a good idea?

....

Vocabulary

4 **These English words from the text all come from Latin. Can you translate them into your language?**

poetry ....

musician ....

elegant ....

reign ....

celebration..

Read

5 **Choose the correct answers to these questions.**

1 When did France become a republic?
   a In 1642.
   b Just over 200 years ago.
   c A hundred years ago.

2 When did the Romans first go to Britain?
   a Nearly 2000 years ago.
   b Nearly 1000 years ago.
   c Nearly 5000 years ago.

3 Who was the first European to sail around the world?
   a The Portuguese explorer, Ferdinand Magellan, in 1519.
   b The English explorer, James Cook, in 1772.
   c The Italian explorer, Christopher Columbus, in 1492.

4 The composer, Frederick Chopin, was:
   a Polish.
   b French.
   c Russian.

5 Who built the Russian city of St Petersburg?
   a Joseph Stalin.
   b Peter The Great.
   c Napoleon.

Write

6 **Write a paragraph about your favourite character in history.**

... was born in (place) in (date) ....
He / She wanted to ... .
He / She became ... .
We remember him / her because ... .

....

Let's check

Vocabulary check

1 **Choose the correct word for each sentence.**

I'm going to count to three and jump …into… the swimming pool.

A into **B** down **C** across

1 How did he get into the house? He climbed .... the window.
A under **B** past **C** through

2 Somebody is walking .... us. Who is it?
A over **B** across **C** towards

3 It's a lovely day. Let's walk .... the path by the river.
A under **B** through **C** along

4 Go .... the bridge and turn right.
A into **B** through **C** over

5 We always walk .... the sweet shop on our way to school.
A past **B** along **C** up

Write your score: ..../10

Grammar check

2 **Match the phrases. Write requests with *Could*.**

Ben's in the bath. [e.] Could you call again in ten minutes?

1 I can't find my dictionary [...] ....
2 It's a lovely day. [...] ....
3 It's cold in here. [...] ....
4 My dog's thirsty. [...] ....
5 My tea is too hot. [...] ....

a you / pass me the milk?
b we / go to the beach?
c I / close the window?
d I / give him some water?
e you / call again in ten minutes?
f you / lend me yours?

Write your score: ..../5

3 **Write sentences with *ago* like the example.**

We saw him at eight o'clock. Now it's ten.
We saw him two hours ago.

1 We bought it on the 12th. Now it's the 15th.
....

2 I called her at 10.15. Now it's 10.45.
....

3 They left the house at 9 o'clock. Now it's 11 o'clock.
....

4 I wrote to her in January. Now it's November.
....

5 She came here on Monday 1st March. Now it's Saturday 13th March.
....

Write your score: ...... /5

4 **Write sentences by putting the words in order**

get / right / roundabout / the / to / Turn / when / you
Turn right when you get to the roundabout.

1 bookshop / Could / me / nearest / tell / the/ the / to / way / you / ?
....
....

2 ago / book / days / I / reading / started / this / three
....
....

3 across / and / He / into the / it / jumped / lake / swam
....
....

4 the bus / get / here / hours / on / It / to / took / two
....
....

5 a / cake / did / your family / for / last / make / When / you / ?
....
....

Write your score: ...... /5

5 **Correct the mistake in each sentence. /\ = there's a word missing; X = change one word; ⤷ = change the order of two words; * = you must delete one word.**

Could pass me the sugar, please? /\
Could you pass me the sugar, please?

1 I started doing this exercise a minute before. **X**
....

2 When did you read last a really funny book? ⤷
....

3 I didn't to buy anything at the museum shop. *
....

4 It was hot, so we sat the tree. /\
....

5 My dog jumped up the gate and ran into the field. **X**
....

Write your score: .... /5

Write your total score: .... /30

How good are you?

★ I'm not very good at this.　★ I'm OK at this.　★★ I'm good at this.

Tick (✓) the correct boxes.

	★	★★	★★★
READING I can understand:			
information about special days — *On Pancake Day we made lots of pancakes.*			
directions and match them to places on a map — *Go along this path. Turn right when you get to the road.*			
a simple newspaper article about a lost ship — *Last year, Giuseppe Russo went swimming …*			
a text about kings and queens of England — *Henry VIII became king at the age of 17.*			
LISTENING I can understand:			
essential information from a conversation — *Alex's birthday meal menu: melon with ham; chicken with onions …*			
directions — *Walk along the path.*			
an account of a discovery — *The ship was very near the beach. It was just three metres away.*			
WRITING I can write:			
about how many things I've got — *I've got lots of CDs. I haven't got many cassettes.*			
about how much I eat/drink — *I eat plenty of fruit. I don't drink much tea.*			
about a special occasion — *I had a brilliant day on my birthday. My friends gave me lots of presents.*			
directions — *Go along Clarence Street and turn right.*			
about a past event from imagination — *Last year I was on holiday and I found a necklace in the sea.*			
SPEAKING I can:			
talk about a special occasion — *We had a great party.*			
ask and answer about past experiences — *What did you do last weekend? My grandparents took me to a football match.*			
talk about special days — *At Hallowe'en we dressed up as witches.*			
talk about when I last did something — *We had a picnic in the forest two weeks ago.*			
make polite requests and answer them — *Could I borrow your mobile phone? Yes, of course.*			
ask for and give directions — *Could you tell me the way to the station? Yes, of course. Turn right and go over the bridge.*			
ask and answer questions from a newspaper article — *Why did the ship sink? Because there was a big storm.*			

Vocabulary groups

Write three more words in each vocabulary group.

Vegetables	onions	carrots	....	....	....
Fruit	orange	apple	....	....	....
Other food	meat	fish	....	....	....

I could do that easily!

Grammar

Past continuous

Reflexive pronouns

would like to + verb

Regular and irregular adverbs

(R) Present simple and Present continuous, revision

(R) Past simple and Past continuous, revision

Vocabulary

Detailed physical description

Personal possessions

Communication

Narrating a story using the Past simple and the Past continuous

Using the phone

Pronunciation

/ɔː/ /ɒ/ /æ/

Culture spot

Britain and America

9

Detailed physical description

1 Talk about five people in your class who have got different hairstyles.

Hairstyle

long

spiky

short

cropped

medium-length

straight

curly

wavy

I've got a beard.

I've got a fringe.

I've got a moustache.

A Alex's got short, spiky hair.

B Julia's got medium-length wavy hair. She's got a fringe.

2 Listen and play 'Simon says'.

Simon says:

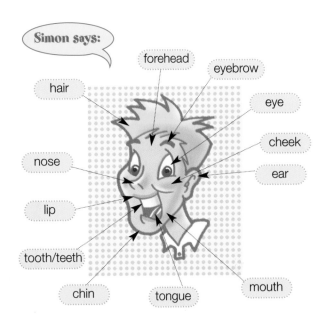

forehead, eyebrow, hair, eye, cheek, nose, ear, lip, tooth/teeth, chin, tongue, mouth

3 Listen and read. Which of the sentences are true for you?

I'm fair-skinned.

I'm dark-skinned.

I've got freckles.

I've got a scar.

I've got a mole.

I've got long nails.

Were you chatting up the boys?

- Past continuous
- Reflexive pronouns
- Narrating a story

🎧 Listen and read

1 **Listen and read.**

Mum	Why are you late home, Kate? Did you miss the bus?
Kate	No, I didn't.
Dad	Were you chatting up the boys again at the bus stop?
Kate	No, I wasn't!
Dad	I was only joking.
Kate	I had to see my teacher after class. That's why I'm late. I got into trouble in the English lesson.
Mum	Why? What were you doing?
Kate	I wasn't doing anything, really. Well, I was reading a magazine under the desk. There was a competition to write a story and we were doing a lesson about how to write a story.
Mum	And you weren't paying attention. What did the teacher say?
Kate	She said, 'You shouldn't read magazines in class.'
Mum	And she gave you a detention.
Kate	Yes, for tomorrow. But I don't care! We were talking about the competition all day at school and we're going to go in for it. The first prize is a day out with Liberty X.

Comprehension

2 **Answer the questions.**

1 Did Kate miss the bus?
 No, she didn't.

2 Why was she late home from school?

3 What was the English lesson about?

4 Is a detention good or bad?

5 What is Kate's plan?

6 What can you win in the competition?

Grammar focus

Past continuous

Affirmative	**Negative**
I was talking.	I wasn't talking.
You were talking.	You weren't talking.
He/She/It was talking.	He/She/It wasn't talking.
We/You/They were talking.	We/You/They weren't talking.

Past continuous = Past simple of *be* + the *ing* form of the verb.

Grammar practice

3 **Look at the dialogue and complete the sentences with *was, wasn't, were* or *weren't*.**

1 Kate ...wasn't....... chatting up boys at the bus stop.

2 Her father .... joking.

3 Kate said, 'I .... doing anything wrong.'

4 Kate and her friends .... doing a lesson about story writing.

5 Kate's mum said, 'You .... paying attention.'

6 They .... talking about the competition at school.

Write

4 Write two sentences for each pair of pictures. Use the phrases in the box and the Past continuous.

do homework	make sandwiches	ski	watch TV
listen to music	play the guitar	snow	~~play a video game~~
make pancakes	rain	snowboard	~~work on the computer~~

1

He _was working on the computer._ He _wasn't playing a video game._

2

I .... I ....

3

We .... We ....

4

You .... You ....

5

They .... They ....

6

It .... It ....

Speak

5a Work in groups. Talk about what you were doing at 5 o'clock yesterday afternoon.

> I was playing a video game.

5b Tell the class what people in your group were doing.

> A Nick was playing a video game.

> B Lisa and Emma were talking on the telephone.

9

6 **Listen and read.**

Mr Evans	Hello, Kate.
Kate	Hello, Mr Evans.
Mr Evans	So you've got a 30-minute detention from your English teacher.
Kate	Yes.
Mr Evans	Were you talking in class?
Kate	No, I wasn't.
Mr Evans	Were you doing your work?
Kate	Well, yes, I was.
Mr Evans	Oh. Well, what were you doing wrong?
Kate	I was reading a magazine under the desk.
Mr Evans	Oh, I see.

CLASS 4A
- FINISH HISTORY PROJECT
- START GRAMMAR EXERCISE
- READ GEOGRAPHY WORKSHEET

Comprehension

7 **Answer the questions.**

1 Where is Kate?
   She's in detention at school.
2 How long must she stay?
3 Who gave her the detention?
4 Why?

Grammar focus

Past continuous

Questions	Short answers	
	Affirmative	**Negative**
Was I reading?	Yes, I was.	No, I wasn't.
Were you reading?	Yes, you were.	No, you weren't.
Was he/she/it reading?	Yes, he/she/it was.	No, he/she/it wasn't.
Were we reading?	Yes, we were.	No, we weren't.
Were you reading?	Yes, you were.	No, you weren't.
Were they reading?	Yes, they were.	No, they weren't.

Grammar practice

8 **Complete the questions and answers.**

1 A .....Was............... he playing in a match?
   B Yes, he ...was...................
2 A .... you waiting to see Mr Evans after school?
   B No, we ....
3 A .... it raining here yesterday?
   B No, it ....
4 A .... you having supper when I phoned?
   B Yes, I ....
5 A .... they looking for their cat?
   B Yes, they ....

Speak

9a **Work with a partner. Ask and answer about Kate's day at school yesterday.**

> **A** Was she chatting up the boys at the bus stop?

> **B** No, she wasn't.

1 What lesson was she doing when she got into trouble?
2 What were the students learning in the lesson?
3 What was Kate reading under the desk?
4 What were she and her friends talking about all day at school?

9b **Now look at Exercise 1 and check your answers.**

Speak

10 Work with a partner. Ask and answer about your partner and his/her family.

How good is your memory?

What were you doing at 6 o'clock yesterday evening?

What were your mum and dad doing?

What was your brother doing?

What was your sister doing?

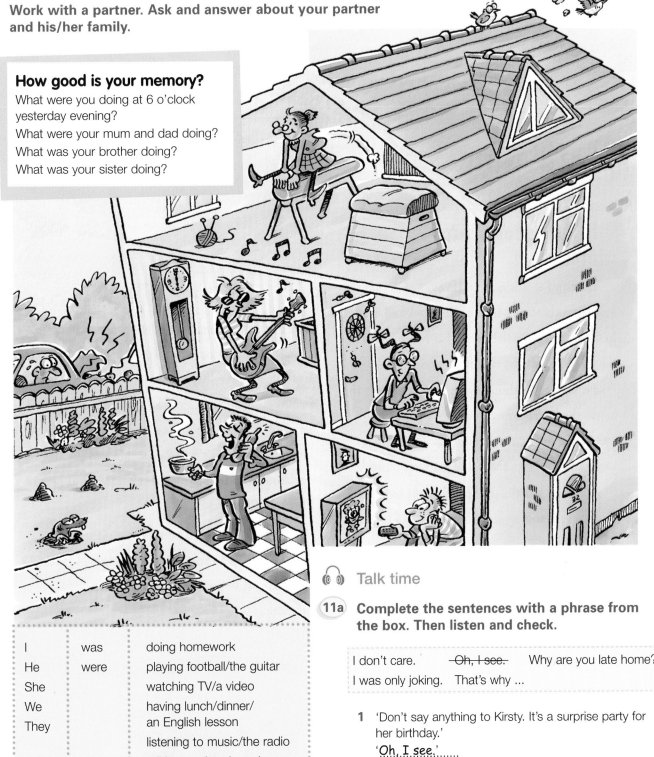

I	was	doing homework
He	were	playing football/the guitar
She		watching TV/a video
We		having lunch/dinner/
They		an English lesson
		listening to music/the radio
		talking on the phone/
		to my friends/to my mum
		and dad
		working on the computer
		reading a book/
		a magazine/a newspaper
		cooking dinner
		chatting up boys/girls
		writing

Talk time

11a Complete the sentences with a phrase from the box. Then listen and check.

I don't care.   ~~Oh, I see.~~   Why are you late home?

I was only joking.   That's why ...

1 'Don't say anything to Kirsty. It's a surprise party for her birthday.'
   'Oh, I see.'

2 It's midnight! ....

3 I wasn't being serious. ....

4 I had a detention. .... I was late home.

5 It's very cold but ....
   I'm going snowboarding anyway.

11b Look at the sentences in Exercise 11a. Which:

• do you say?

• do your brothers and sisters say?

• do your parents/teachers say?

🎧 Listen and read

12 Listen and read the story.

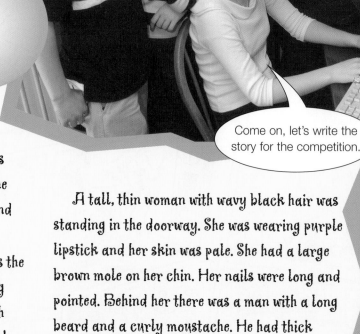

Come on, let's write the story for the competition.

Bat's-wing Soup

It was a cold, dark winter night.

The wind was whistling through the trees and the owls were hooting. Annabel had one last newspaper to deliver to the house behind the tall trees at the end of the road.

As she was walking up the path towards the house she heard some strange noises. A dog was howling. A cat was screeching. A witch was cackling! No, she was imagining things!

'Don't be silly!' Annabel thought to herself. But there it was again! She walked up to the door.

As she was putting the newspaper through the door ... it opened.

A tall, thin woman with wavy black hair was standing in the doorway. She was wearing purple lipstick and her skin was pale. She had a large brown mole on her chin. Her nails were long and pointed. Behind her there was a man with a long beard and a curly moustache. He had thick eyebrows and long, wavy black hair. And he had black teeth.

'Come in!' said the woman in a deep voice. 'Help yourself to some bat's-wing soup. I made it myself. But be careful, it's hot. Don't burn yourself.'

Comprehension

13 Put the pictures in the order of the story.

1 .....d.....

Grammar focus

Reflexive pronouns

Subject pronouns	Reflexive pronouns
I	myself
you	yourself
he	himself
she	herself
it	itself
we	ourselves
you	yourselves
they	themselves

How many reflexive pronouns can you find in the story?

Grammar practice

14 **Complete the sentences with the correct reflexive pronouns.**

1 OK, everybody. The sandwiches are in the kitchen, so I want all of you to help ..yourselves...

2 They really enjoyed .... at the party.

3 No, I'm not going to tidy your room for you. Do it .... !

4 'She fell off her bike.'
'Did she hurt ....?'

5 'Do you need any help with your homework?'
'It's OK, thanks. I can do it ....'

6 'Did Harry's mother pay for your tickets?'
'No, we paid for them ....'

7 Does your computer switch .... off automatically?

 Pronunciation

/ɔː/ and /ɒ/

15a **Listen and repeat.**

/ɔː/	/ɒ/
talk	dog
for	long
door	hot

15b **Write the words below in the correct column. Then listen and check.**

tall	story	your
stop	blonde	wrong

 Extra!

16 **Work in groups. Tell the story. Listen again to how Kate and her friends do it.**

 Listen

17 **Listen and say which ending you like best, Sophie's, Kate's, Ashan's or Alex's.**

Write

18 **Write a description of a character in a film.**

Hagrid is tall and very big. He's got long, black wavy hair and dark brown eyes.

Extra!

19 **Write your own ending for the story. What did Annabel do next? Add your work to your Portfolio.**

Skills development

My most **embarrassing** moment

Read

1 Read the sentences and put them in the order of the pictures to make a story.

☐	I flew through the air and landed on a bench where a woman was sitting. She was eating an ice cream.
☐	I knocked into her.
☐	I didn't hurt myself but the ice cream went all over her nose and chin.
☐	I was winning.
1	On holiday last year, my brother and I were having a race on our bikes.
☐	When I looked behind me to see my brother, I crashed into a litter bin.

2 **Listen and complete the text with the missing words. They're all parts of the body.**

I was having a ....**tooth**...... out at the dentist's.
Suddenly I felt a sharp pain in my ....
My .... shot up quickly and hit the
dentist in the .... I knocked him right
off his .... And he pulled my
.... out at the same time!

Speak

3 **Work with a partner. Take turns to tell a funny story using the words and phrases in the table.**

Say where you were.	be	in the park at school at home	I was in the park with my friends.
Say what you were doing.	have watch play	a picnic football lunch TV	We were having a picnic.
Say what happened.	see drop throw	a big dog the ball a spider my sandwich my ice cream	Suddenly I saw a big dog. I dropped my sandwich.
Say how the story ended.			The dog ate it. The dog ran off with it. (It went all over the floor.) (It hit a teacher on the head.)

Write

4 **Now write your partner's story.**

Jack was at the swimming pool with his brother .....

Let's check

Vocabulary check

1 **Complete each sentence with the correct word.**

cheeks	forehead	scar
chin	glasses	short
curly	~~mouth~~	teeth
eyes	fair	

"Are you eating a sweet?" "No. I've got chewing gum in my ....**mouth**........ ."

1 Are you hot? You've got pink ....

2 I can't see the board. I'm not wearing my .... today.

3 I clean my .... after every meal.

4 I fell off my bike two years ago and I've still got a .... on my hand.

5 Shut your .... and go to sleep.

6 The opposite of dark-skinned is ....-skinned.

7 The opposite of long is ....

8 The opposite of straight hair is ....hair.

9 You can't see her .... because she's got a fringe.

10 You can't see his .... because he's got a big beard.

Write your score: ..../10

Grammar check

2 **Choose the correct word for each sentence.**

Look at that dog in the water. It's really enjoying ...**itself**.... .

A herself   **B** themselves   (**C** itself)

1 Help .... to a biscuit.
A himself   **B** themselves   **C** yourself

2 We didn't enjoy .... at the party. It was boring.
A yourself   **B** themselves   **C** ourselves

3 Don't make me a sandwich. I'll make it ....
A myself   **B** itself   **C** herself

4 I didn't help them with the dinner. They made it ....
A itself   **B** themselves   **C** yourselves

5 He's very good at music. He wrote this song ....
A himself   **B** herself   **C** itself

Write your score: ..../5

3 **Choose the correct words for each sentence.**

Were you. listening in class this morning?
A Did you   **B** Was you   (**C** Were you)

1 At three o'clock yesterday we .... tennis.
A play   **B** was playing   **C** were playing

2 What .... this morning?
A you are doing   **B** were doing   **C** were you doing

3 I .... laughing at you.
A wasn't   **B** weren't   **C** didn't

4 Where .... waiting for them?
A was she   **B** she was   **C** did she

5 They .... videos at my house last night.
A watching   **B** were watching   **C** watch

Write your score: ..../5

4 **Write sentences in the Past continuous.**

We (sit) in the park.
We were sitting in the park.

1 What (you and Joey/ talk) about just now?
....

2 At five o'clock we (watch) a film called *Day of the Dog.*
....

3 She (not think) and she told him about the party.
....

4 (they / wait) for you outside the cinema?
....

5 Who (you /play) tennis with on Saturday?
....

Write your score: .... /5

5 **Correct the mistake in each sentence. /\ = there's a word missing; X = change one word; ↳ = change the order of two words; * = you must delete one word.**

My sister made that soup himself. **X**
My sister made that soup herself.

1 They didn't enjoy themself at the carnival. **X**
....

2 She wearing purple lipstick at the Hallowe'en party. /\
....

3 Why he was sitting in that cold, dark room? ↳
....

4 They wasn't raining yesterday afternoon. **X**
....

5 What time were you doing in town yesterday? *
....

Write your score: .... /5
Write your total score: .... /35

10

Personal possessions

1 Listen and write the numbers of the things Max and Claire have got. 🎧

Max   1,................
Claire   4,................

1 sunglasses ☐

2 mobile phone ☐

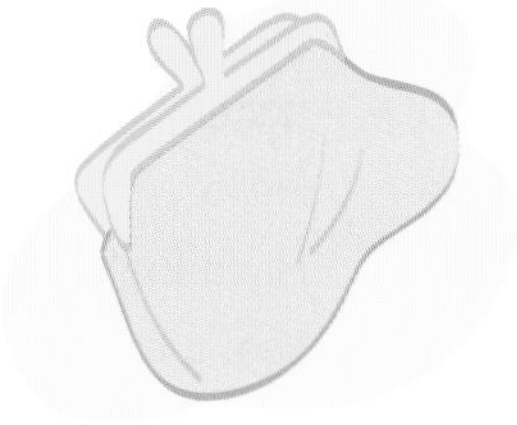

3 diary ☐

4 purse ☐

5 key ring ☐

6 comb ☐

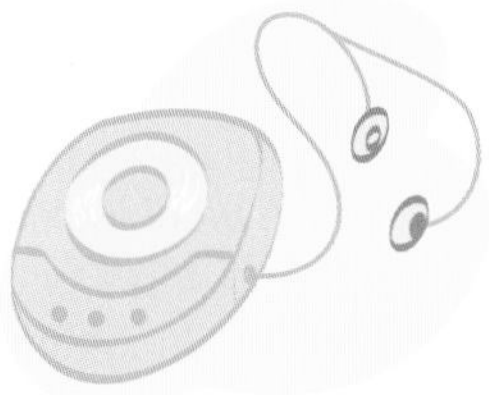

7 personal CD player ☐

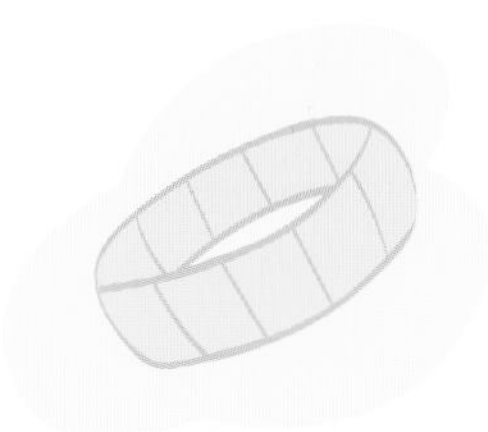

8 bracelet ☐

9 earring ☐

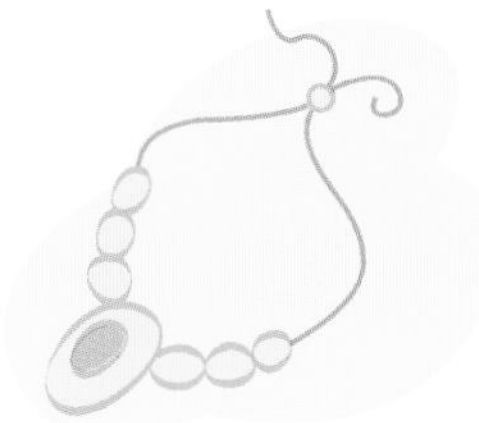

10 necklace ☐

11 watch ☐

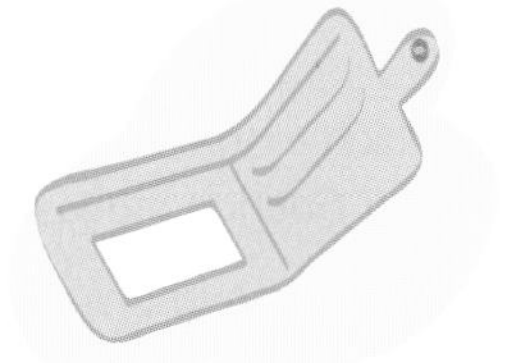

12 wallet ☐

13 camera ☐

14 skateboard ☐

2 Tick (✓) the things you've got.

3 Work with a partner. Tell your partner what you've got. Your partner must write the numbers.

I've got some sunglasses. I've got ...

Would you like to meet Liberty X?

- *would like to* + **verb**
- **Regular and irregular adverbs**
- **Present simple and Present continuous, revision**
- **Past simple and Past continuous, revision**
- **Using the phone**

Listen and read

1 **Listen and read.**

Linda Hi, could I speak to Kate Campbell, please?

Mum Sorry, she isn't here. Can I take a message? ... Ah, that's her now. Could you hold on? Kate, it's for you. It's someone with an American accent.

Kate Hello.

Linda Hi. Is that Kate?

Kate Yes, it is.

Linda My name's Linda. I'm phoning from *Top Sounds* magazine. I have some great news for you. You and your friends are the winners of our competition!

Kate Really?

Linda We just loved your story. We were looking for something really different. And yours was the best because it was so funny. Congratulations!

Kate Oh, thank you.

Linda We're going to give each of you a personal CD player. And Liberty X are making a video in London next Saturday. Would you like to meet them?

Kate Yes, we'd love to. It sounds great!

Comprehension

2 **Answer the questions.**

1 Which magazine does Linda work for?
   <u>Top Sounds magazine</u>

2 Why is she phoning?

3 Why was Bat's-Wing Soup the best story?

4 What did Kate and her friends win?

5 What's happening next Saturday?

Grammar focus

would like to + **verb**

Would you like to go to the cinema on Saturday?
Yes, **I would**./Yes, **I'd** love to.
I'm sorry, I'm afraid I can't.

What **would you like to do** on your birthday?
I'd like to have a party.

Find examples of this structure in the dialogue.

Grammar practice

3 **Complete the dialogues.**

1 **A** Would you like .....<u>to</u>......... play tennis on Saturday?

   B Yes, ... love to.

2 **A** What .... you like to do at the weekend?

   B .... you like to go for a bike ride?

3 **A** .... you and Chloe like to come to my house after school?

   B I'm sorry, I'm afraid we can't.

4 **A** Would you .... to try a piece of my chocolate cake?

   B Yes, I .... Thanks.

Pronunciation

/æ/ and /ʌ/

4a **Listen and repeat.**

1	sun	**3**	up	**5**	lunch
2	club	**4**	funny	**6**	run

4b **Now listen to these pairs of words.**

	/æ/	/ʌ/
1	cap	cup
2	bat	but
3	cat	cut
4	ran	run
5	match	much

4c **Work with a partner. Say one of the words in each pair. Your partner decides which word you said.**

Speak

5 **Work with a partner. Ask and answer questions using the phrases in the box.**

> **A** What would you like to do at the weekend?

> **B** I'd like to go to the cinema.

Questions	Answers
at the weekend?	have a barbecue
for your next birthday?	have a party
in the summer holidays?	have some friends round
	play (football) in the park
	go out for a meal
	go to the beach
	go to the cinema
	go to (America)
	go camping
	go to the seaside

 Talk time

6a **Listen and read.**

> **A** Hello, could I speak to Gabriella, please?

> **B** Yes, hold on, I'll get her for you. She's in her room.

> **A** Thanks.

> **A** Hello, could I speak to Carlo please?

> **B** I'm sorry. He isn't here. He's playing football. Can I take a message?

> **A** Yes, please. Could you say Luca phoned. And I'll phone him tomorrow.

6b **Role-play the phone dialogues below. Use Exercise 6a to help you.**

1 Dracula calls Frankenstein. Frankenstein isn't in. He's walking in the forest.

2 The Prince calls Cinderella. One of her sisters answers. Cinderella is in. She's doing the washing-up in the kitchen.

3 James Bond calls Special Agent 006. Special Agent 006 isn't in. He's skiing in the mountains.

 Extra!

6c **Memorize and act out your phone dialogues.**

Listen and read

7 **Listen and read.**

It's Saturday. Kate and her friends are at the studios watching Liberty X.

Sophie	This is fantastic. I can't believe we're here.
Ashan	They learn the dance steps quickly.
Kate	I know. And they dance so well. How do they do it?
Ashan	They work hard.
Alex	I could do that easily.
Kate	Alex, you can't sing and you dance like a donkey!
Alex	I don't! I'm a good dancer. Look!
All	Alex!

Comprehension

8 **Answer the questions.**

1 What day is it? <u>It's Saturday.</u>
2 Where are Kate and her friends?
3 Who are they watching?
4 What do they think of the dancing?
5 Do they think Alex is a good dancer?

Grammar focus

Adverbs
Regular adverbs

To make regular adverbs, add *ly* to the adjectives:

quick   quick**ly**

If the adjective ends in *y,* change the *y* to *i* and add *ly:*

easy   eas**ily**

Irregular adverbs

These adjectives have irregular adverbs:

Adjective	**Adverb**
good	well
hard	hard
fast	fast
early	early
late	late

Which of these adverbs are irregular in your language?

Grammar practice

9 **Make the adjectives into adverbs and use them to complete the sentences.**

safe	fast	quiet
~~slow~~	good	early

1 I could understand Sasha because he spoke ..slowly................

2 You did .... in your exams. Congratulations!

3 It was a dangerous journey but they arrived ....

4 It was after midnight, so they went into the house ....

5 We were late for school, so we cycled very ....

6 She left school .... because she had a doctor's appointment.

Read and speak

10a **Work with a partner. Tick (✓) the sentences which describe you. Then tick (✓) the sentences which describe your partner.**

How well do you know yourself?

Me	My partner
I ...	He/She ...
• dance well.	• dances well.
• sing well.	• sings well.
• learn dance routines quickly.	• learns dance routines quickly.
• stay up late at weekends.	• stays up late at weekends.
• always get up early.	• always gets up early.
• do my hair carefully.	• does his/her hair carefully.
• can run very fast.	• can run very fast.
• speak quietly.	• speaks quietly.
• work hard at school.	• works hard at school.
• usually get to school early.	• usually gets to school early.
• speak English well.	• speaks English well.
• always listen carefully.	• always listens carefully.

10b **Read out the sentences which you think describe your partner. Does your partner agree?**

A I think you dance well.

B That's true.

A I think you learn dance routines quickly.

B That's not true.

> **Remember!** To ask who something belongs to, use *whose*: **Whose** key ring is this? / Whose is this key ring? **Whose** bracelets are these? / Whose are these bracelets?

Speak

11 **Work with a partner. Ask and answer about these items.**

A Whose sunglasses are these?

B They're Alex's.

A Whose is this purse?

B It's ....

1

2

3

4

5

6

7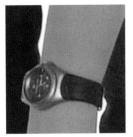

8

TEMPO QUIZ
How much can you remember ?

12 Choose a sentence from each column to describe the photos.

1 .They were in a department store. Kate was buying a pig. They saw Alex and Ashan.

2 ....

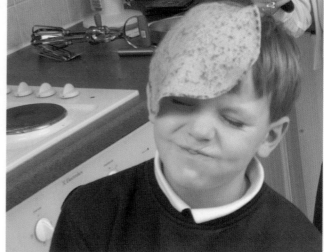

3 ....

4 ....

Where were they?	What were they doing?	What happened next?
They were at Ashan's house.	Kate was buying a pink pig.	Jamie threw one at Kate.
They were at the railway station.	They were cooking sausages.	Ashan cooked pizzas.
They were in a field.	They were doing a sponsored walk.	They burnt them.
They were in a department store.	They were doing their Geography homework.	They had a picnic in the garden.
They were in the kitchen.	They were going to Hampton Court Palace.	They raised £100 for the hospital.
They were near Holkham Beach.	They were making pancakes.	They saw Alex and Ashan.

5 ....

6 ....

Bye

Portfolio

13 Write an e-mail to a new pen-friend. Describe your appearance and character and tell him/her about your interests. Go to page 132.

Skills development

A rap artist

Bow Wow

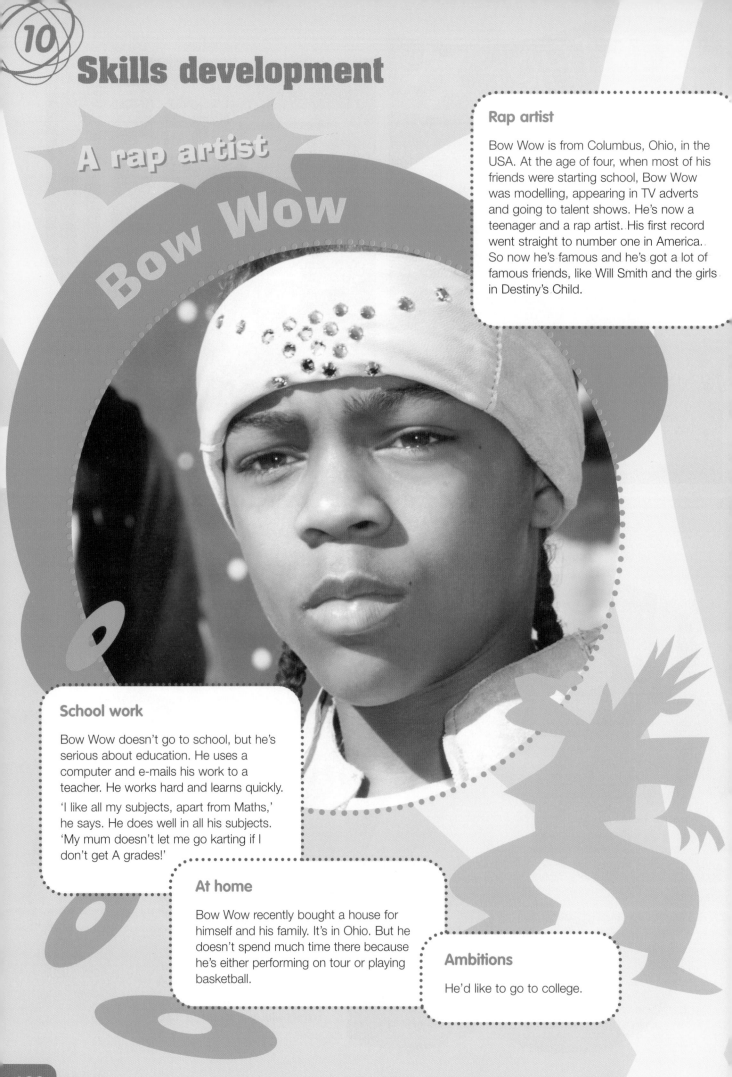

Rap artist

Bow Wow is from Columbus, Ohio, in the USA. At the age of four, when most of his friends were starting school, Bow Wow was modelling, appearing in TV adverts and going to talent shows. He's now a teenager and a rap artist. His first record went straight to number one in America. So now he's famous and he's got a lot of famous friends, like Will Smith and the girls in Destiny's Child.

School work

Bow Wow doesn't go to school, but he's serious about education. He uses a computer and e-mails his work to a teacher. He works hard and learns quickly.

'I like all my subjects, apart from Maths,' he says. He does well in all his subjects. 'My mum doesn't let me go karting if I don't get A grades!'

At home

Bow Wow recently bought a house for himself and his family. It's in Ohio. But he doesn't spend much time there because he's either performing on tour or playing basketball.

Ambitions

He'd like to go to college.

Read

1 Read about Bow Wow. Then write the correct words in the spaces to find out the name of his most famous fan.

1 It isn't his favourite school subject.
2 His nationality.
3 They are his friends.
4 He bought a house in ....
5 His first record was ... one in the USA.
6 Does he go to school? ..., he doesn't.
7 His mum would like him to get ... grades.

M	A	T	H	S								
					'							

Listen

2a Listen to Bow Wow's fans talking about him and complete the notes.

Age: ....
Birthday: ....
He started rapping when he was: ....
He lives in: ....
His house has got: _a karting track_.....................
....
Free-time activities: ....
....
....

2b Listen again. What's the disadvantage for Bow Wow of being famous?

Speak

3 Work with a partner. Role-play an interview with Bow Wow. Use the information on page 122 and the notes you made in Exercise 2a.

A   B

1 How old are you?   I'm 15.
2 When's your birthday?
3 What were you doing when you were four years old?
4 When did you start rapping?
5 Where do you live?
6 Which school subjects do you like?
7 What do you do in your free time?
8 What would you like to do in the future?

Write

4 Are you like Bow Wow? Read the sentences below and write similar ones about yourself.

Bow Wow
1 I don't like Maths.
2 I work hard and I learn quickly.
3 I haven't got many friends of my own age.
4 I've got a lot of famous friends.
5 I don't watch much TV in my free time.
6 I play basketball and I go karting.
7 I'd like to go to college in the future.

Me
1 I like Maths but I don't like History.
2 ....
3 ....
4 ....
5 ....
6 ....
7 ....

Speak

5 Work with a partner. Talk about yourself using the sentences you wrote in Exercise 4.

A I like Maths but I don't like History.

B I don't like Maths or History. I like English.

Culture spot

Britain and America

Read and write

1   **Britain or America – which is it and how do you know? Write** *Britain* **and** *America* **in the correct places. Then complete the sentences about your country.**

1

This is ……….……….............. .

In Britain you drive on the left.

This is ……….……….............. .

In America you drive on the right.

In my country, ………………………………………………………………………………………........................

2

This is ……….……….............. .

The Statue of Liberty is a famous monument in New York.

This is ……….……….............. .

Big Ben is a famous monument in London.

…………………………………… **is a famous monument in my country. It's in** …………………………………

3

This is ……….……….............. .

Britain has a queen.

This is ……….……….............. .

America has a president.

My country ………………………………………………………………………………………........................

2 **Complete the chart.**

	The United Kingdom	The USA	My country
Area	244,820 km^2	9,629,091 km^2	....
Capital	....	Washington DC	....
Population	59,778,000	280,562,489	....
Head of state	Queen Elizabeth II	}	....
Head of government	....		....
Currency	the pound (sterling)	....	....
Tourist features	The Tower of London Big Ben Buckingham Palace Edinburgh Castle The Lake District	Disney World The Grand Canyon The Statue of Liberty Yellowstone National Park	....

Vocabulary

3 **Listen to the dialogues. Find a word or phrase in the box for each American English word or phrase.**

British English

- jumper
- chemist's
- mobile phone
- football
- chips
- shopping centre
- crisps
- ~~biscuit~~
- cinema
- trainers

American English	British English
1 cookie	..biscuit..........................
2 French fries	....
3 potato chips	....
4 movie theater	....
5 soccer	....
6 cell phone	....
7 mall	....
8 sweater	....
9 sneakers	....
10 pharmacy	....

Write

4 **Read about the Empire State Building. Find interesting facts and figures about another famous building. Write a similar profile.**

- This is the Empire State Building. It's in New York. It was built in 1931.
- It's got 102 floors. On the 86th floor, there's an outdoor observatory. Boy Scouts and Girl Guides can go to a special camp there. There's also an observatory at the top of the building, on the 102nd floor. The view is fantastic.
- Every year there's a race to the top of the building. You start at the bottom and run up all the stairs. It takes nearly ten minutes for the fastest runners!

Let's check

Vocabulary check

1 **Match the personal possessions to the clues.**

bracelet	earring	sunglasses
~~camera~~	key ring	wallet
comb	mobile phone	watch
diary	purse	

You use it to take pictures. ..camera...........................

1 You can use it to call your friends. ....

2 You can put your money in this. ....

3 ... or in this ....

4 You should wear them in the sun. ....

5 You write important things in it. ....

6 You use it to tidy your hair. ....

7 You need one to know the time. ....

8 You put your keys on it. ....

9 You wear it in your ear. ....

10 You wear it on your arm. ....

Write your score: ..../10

Grammar check

2 **Put the correct verb in the correct tense: Past simple or Past continuous.**

They (open / do) their homework when the door suddenly (open / do).
They were doing their homework when the door suddenly opened.

1 She (hear / have) a shower when she (hear / have) the telephone.

....

....

2 How fast (he run / he fall) when he (run / fall)?

....

....

3 I (meet / walk) up the street when I (meet / walk) Amy.

....

....

4 We (find / go) to the shops when we (find / go) £10.

....

....

5 Where (you sit / you see) when you (sit / see) the ghost?

....

....

Write your score: ..../5

3 **Choose the correct adverb for each sentence.**

fast	late	quietly	~~early~~	slowly	well

We must get up ....early...... tomorrow morning. The bus leaves at six.

1 I don't know a lot of English. Please speak

....

2 I'm not very good at sport and I can't run very

....

3 Please speak ....
My little brother is asleep.

4 He's brilliant at music. He plays the guitar really

....

5 He always gets up .... on Sunday morning.

Write your score: ..../5

4 **Choose the correct words for each sentence.**

Where did you ....find. your earring?

A found   **B** find   **C** finding

1 Would you like .... my holiday photos?

A to see   **B** see   **C** seeing

2 Where .... this CD?

A were you   **B** you bought   **C** did you buy buying

3 We .... a great film on TV last night.

A see   **B** were seeing   **C** saw

4 ... you need any help with the cooking?

A Are   **B** Do   **C** Were

5 She didn't ... off the computer last night.

A switch   **B** switched   **C** switching

6 ... he wearing an earring?

A Did   **B** Was   **C** Does

7 My mother never ... my room for me.

A is tidying   **B** tidies   **C** was tidying

8 ... you like to come to our Hallowe'en party?

A Did   **B** Are   **C** Would

9 ... talking on the phone a minute ago?

A Were you   **B** Did you   **C** Are you

10 He ... miss the bus last night.

A won't   **B** doesn't   **C** didn't

Write your score: ..../10

Write your score: ..../30

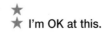

How good are you?

★ I'm not very good at this.   ★★ I'm OK at this.   ★★★ I'm good at this.

Tick (✓) the correct boxes.

READING I can understand:		★	★★	★★★
words from context with the help of illustrations	A dog was howling … a cat was screeching			
a simple story about an embarrassing moment	We were having a race on our bikes. I was winning …			
an article about a teenage rap artist	… he's famous and he's got a lot of famous friends, like Will Smith…			
a text about differences between Britain and the USA	In Britain you drive on the left and in America you drive on the right.			

LISTENING I can understand:				
words from context with the help of sound effects	A witch was cackling …			
a simple horror story	… there was a fire one Hallowe'en and …			
a simple story about an embarrassing moment	I was having a tooth out at the dentist's. Suddenly I felt a sharp pain …			
a conversation about a famous teenage rap artist	What's his house like? It's got a karting track in the garden and it's got …			
from context the meaning of some common American English words	Would you like a cookie with your coffee?			

WRITING I can write:				
about what people were doing	He was working on the computer.			
a description of a character in a film	Harry Potter has got dark hair and he wears glasses.			
a short funny story	Mark was walking in the park with his dog. Suddenly the dog …			

SPEAKING I can:				
talk about what I/a friend was doing	I was making pancakes. Alex was talking on the phone.			
tell a funny story	Some people were having a picnic in the park. I kicked a ball and it went into their lunch.			
ask and answer about plans for the future	What would you like to do at the weekend? I'd like to go camping.			
have simple phone conversations	Hello, could I speak to Carlo, please?			
describe abilities	I dance well. Maria speaks quietly.			
role-play an interview with a rap artist	What would you like to do in the future? I'd like to go to college.			

Vocabulary groups

Write five more words in each vocabulary group.

Hair   long   short   ....

Face   eye   nose   ....

1 **Complete the chart.**

	Me	My best friend	My (dad/mum)
Name			
Age			
Favourite sports and activities			
Favourite food			
Favourite shops			
Personality			

2 **Now write a personal profile about the three people using the information in the chart.**

My name is ....
I'm 12 years old. ....
I like swimming. ....

My best friend's name is ....
He's .... years old.
He likes ....
His favourite food is ....
His favourite shops are ....
He's (quite clever) and he's (very funny).

Module 2   An e-mail about a day out

1 Look on the internet and find out what the weather is going to be like next weekend.

2 Write an e-mail to a friend.

- Suggest going out for a day on Saturday
- Say what the weather's going to be like
- Suggest some things you can do

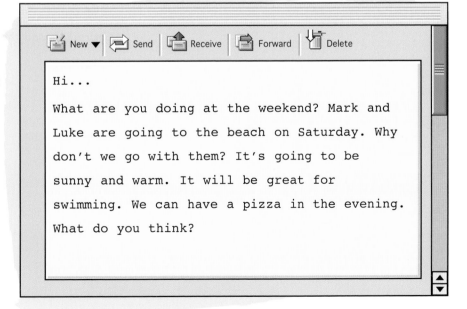

New ▾ | Send | Receive | Forward | Delete

Hi...

What are you doing at the weekend? Mark and Luke are going to the beach on Saturday. Why don't we go with them? It's going to be sunny and warm. It will be great for swimming. We can have a pizza in the evening. What do you think?

1 **Give an example of each of the following types of programme.**

the news ....
the weather ....
a comedy programme ....
a cartoon ....
a film ....
a sports programme ....

a soap opera ....
a documentary ....
a nature programme ....
a quiz show ....
a music programme ....
the adverts ....

2 **Ask and answer:**

What's your favourite...

comedy programme? ....

cartoon? ....

soap opera? ....

nature programme? ....

quiz show? ....

music programme? ....

advert? ....

3 **Which is the most popular comedy programme, cartoon, etc. in your class?**

The most popular comedy programme is ....
....

4 **Write a review for your school magazine describing an interesting film or TV programme. Include information on:**

- when you saw it
- the main characters
- the story
- give your opinion of the film.

I saw *Lord of the Rings* last week. It's about a magic ring. The main characters are a hobbit called Frodo and a wizard called Gandalf. Frodo also has a friend called Sam. Gandalf helps Frodo and Sam on their dangerous journey with the ring. It's a long film but it's fantastic. The battle scenes are incredible and the special effects are excellent.

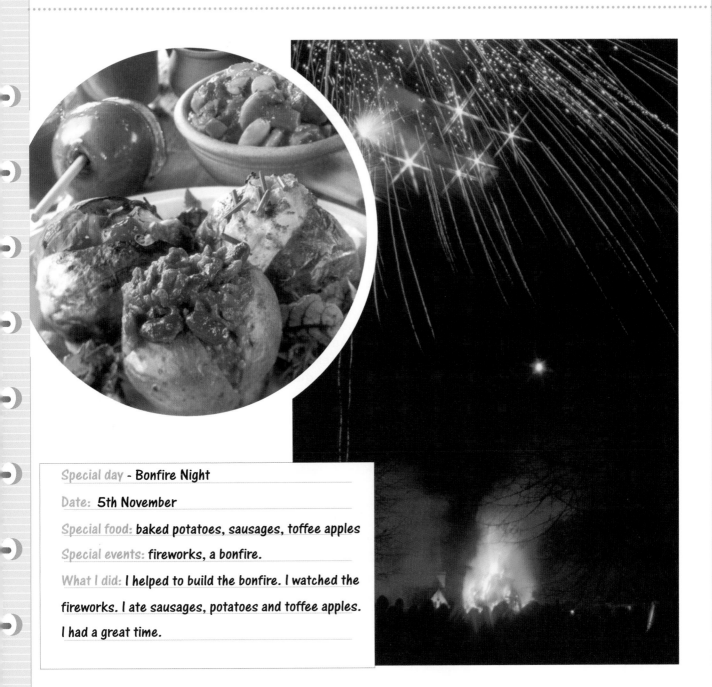

Special day - **Bonfire Night**

Date: **5th November**

Special food: **baked potatoes, sausages, toffee apples**

Special events: **fireworks, a bonfire.**

What I did: **I helped to build the bonfire. I watched the fireworks. I ate sausages, potatoes and toffee apples. I had a great time.**

1 **Write similar information about your special day.**

2 **Now write an article for your school magazine about your special day.**

On November 5th I went to my friend's house and I helped to build a big bonfire for Bonfire Night. In the evening, my parents came and brought lots of fireworks. We cooked sausages and potatoes in the fire and we also ate toffee apples. We had a great time.

1   **Read the e-mail from Iona.**

New ▼ | Send | Receive | Forward | Delete

Hi!

My name's Iona. I live in Perth, in Scotland.
I'm 13 years old and I go to Perth High School.

I'm quite tall. I've got reddish-brown hair and I've got a
fringe. I've got green eyes. I'm quite sporty and I like
telling jokes, so my friends say I'm funny. But I'm
sometimes shy.

I like athletics and swimming and I go to dance classes on
Saturday mornings. I like music and I'm learning to play
the flute. I love going to the cinema and I love animals.
I've got a cat called Cassius. He's quite naughty but he's
very funny.

Send me an e-mail and tell me about yourself.

Bye for now,

Iona

2   **Now write a reply to Iona's e-mail. Include information about:**

- your age, nationality and school
- your appearance
- your personality
- your interests.

Sing a song

LADY
by Modjo

1 Work with a partner. Try to guess the missing words.

Lady, hear .... tonight

'Cause my feeling .... just so right

As .... dance by the moonlight

Can't you see you're .... delight

Lady, ... just feel like

I .... get you out of my mind

I feel love for the .... time

And I know that .... is true

I can tell by the look in .... eyes

(Repeat)

* 'Cause = because

2 Now listen to the song. See if you were correct.

3 Sing the song.

Sing a song

Reach
by S Club

1 **Read the song. Then listen to it.**

When the world leaves you feeling blue
You can count on me, I will be there for you
When it seems all your hopes and dreams
Are a million miles away, I will reassure you

We've got to all stick together
Good friends, there for each other
Never ever forget that
I've got you and you've got me, so

Chorus
Reach for the stars
Climb every mountain higher
Reach for the stars
Follow your heart's desire
Reach for the stars
And when that rainbow's shining over you
That's when your dreams will all come true

There's a place waiting just for you
It's a special place where your dreams all come true
Fly away, swim the ocean blue
Drive that open road, leave the past behind you
Don't stop, gotta keep moving
Your hopes have gotta keep building
Never ever forget that
I've got you and you've got me, so

(Repeat chorus)

Don't believe in all that you've been told
The sky's the limit, you can reach your goal
No-one knows just what the future holds
There ain't nothing you can't be
There's a whole world at your feet
I said reach

Climb every mountain (reach)
Reach for the moon (reach)
Follow the rainbow
And your dreams will all come true

(Repeat chorus twice)

gotta = have got to

ain't = isn't

2 **Match the phrases from the song with their meanings.**

1 I'm feeling blue. ....1d........
2 You can count on me.
3 I will reassure you.
4 We've got to all stick together.
5 Follow your heart's desire.
6 Leave the past behind you.
7 The sky's the limit.
8 There's a whole world at your feet.

a Do what you want to do.
b Everything is possible.
c I'll be there to tell you everything is OK.
d I'm unhappy.
e There are lots of opportunities for you.
f Think about the present and the future.
g We must help each other.
h You can depend on me.

3 **Learn the chorus and sing along.**

Irregular verbs

Infinitive	Past simple	Infinitive	Past simple
be	was/were	let	let
become	became	lose	lost
begin	began	make	made
bite	bit	meet	met
break	broke	pay	paid
bring	brought	put	put
build	built	read /riːd/	read /red/
burn	burned/burnt	ride	rode
buy	bought	ring	rang
catch	caught	run	ran
choose	chose	say	said
come	came	see	saw
cost	cost	send	sent
cut	cut	shoot	shot
do	did	shut	shut
drink	drank	sing	sang
drive	drove	sink	sank
eat	ate	sit	sat
fall	fell	sleep	slept
feel	felt	speak	spoke
find	found	spend	spent
fly	flew	stand	stood
forget	forgot	swim	swam
get	got	swing	swung
give	gave	take	took
go	went	teach	taught
have	had	tell	told
hear	heard	think	thought
hit	hit	throw	threw
hold	held	understand	understood
keep	kept	wake up	woke up
know	knew	wear	wore
learn	learned/learnt	win	won
leave	left	write	wrote

A

about	/əˈbaʊt/
about ▶ What about …?	/əˈbaʊt/ /wɒt əˈbaʊt…/
accent	/ˈæksənt/
across	/əˈkrɒs/
active	/ˈæktɪv/
activity	/ækˈtɪvɪtɪ/
actor	/ˈæktə(r)/
addition ▶ in addition to	/əˈdɪʃn/ /ɪn əˈdɪʃn tə/
advert/advertisement	/ˈædvɜːt/ /ədˈvɜːtɪsmənt/
afraid ▶ I'm afraid …	/əˈfreɪd/ /aɪm əˈfreɪd/
after	/ˈɑːftə(r)/
afternoon	/ˌɑːftəˈnuːn/
afterwards	/ˈɑːftəwədz/
again	/əˈgen/
against	/əˈgenst/
agent	/ˈeɪdʒənt/
ages ▶ for ages	/ˈeɪdʒɪz/ /fə(r) ˈeɪdʒɪz/
ago	/əˈgəʊ/
air	/eə(r)/
airport	/ˈeəpɔːt/
album	/ˈælbəm/
all	/ɔːl/
all over ▶ It went all over the floor.	/ɔːl ˈəʊvə/ /ɪt went ˌɔːl əʊvə ðə ˈflɔː(r)/
all right	/ɔːl ˈraɪt/
alone	/əˈləʊn/
along	/əˈlɒŋ/
always	/ˈɔːlweɪz/
ambition	/æmˈbɪʃn/
ancient	/ˈeɪnʃənt/
angry	/ˈæŋgrɪ/
animal	/ˈænɪməl/
annoying	/əˈnɔɪɪŋ/
another	/əˈnʌðə(r)/
answer	/ˈɑːnsə(r)/
anything, not … anything	/ˈenɪθɪŋ/ /nɒt … ˈenɪθɪŋ/
Anyway, …	/ˈenɪweɪ/
apart from	/əˈpɑːt frəm/
anywhere ▶ I didn't see (her) anywhere	/ˈenɪweə(r)/ /aɪ dɪdnt siː hɜː(r) ˈenɪweə(r)/
appear	/əˈpɪə(r)/
appearance	/əˈpɪərəns/
apple	/ˈæpl/
appointment	/əˈpɔɪntmənt/
area	/ˈeərɪə/
arm	/ɑːm/
arrive	/əˈraɪv/
artist	/ˈɑːtɪst/
as	/æz, əz/
asleep	/əˈsliːp/
ask	/ɑːsk/
ate ◀ eat	/eɪt, iːt/
athletics	/æθˈletɪks/
attention ▶ pay attention	/əˈtenʃn/ /peɪ əˈtenʃn/
audition	/ɔːˈdɪʃn/
aunt	/ɑːnt/
automatically	/ˌɔːtəˈmætɪklɪ/
awake	/əˈweɪk/

B

back ▶ be back	/bæk/ /bɪ ˈbæk/
back ▶ have back	/bæk/ /hæv ˈbæk/
back	/bæk/
bad	/bæd/
badge	/bædʒ/
bag	/bæg/
bakery	/ˈbeɪkərɪ/
banana	/bəˈnɑːnə/
band	/bænd/
barbecue	/ˈbɑːbɪkjuː/
bark	/bɑːk/
basketball	/ˈbɑːskɪtbɔːl/
bat	/bæt/
bath	/bɑːθ/
bathroom	/ˈbɑːθruːm/
beach	/biːtʃ/
bean	/biːn/

beard	/ˈbɪəd/
beautiful	/ˈbjuːtɪfʊl/
became ◀ become	/bɪˈkeɪm, bɪˈkʌm/
because	/bɪˈkʌz/
become	/bɪˈkʌm/
bed	/bed/
bedtime	/ˈbedtaɪm/
beef	/biːf/
before	/bɪˈfɔː(r)/
behind	/bɪˈhaɪnd/
believe	/bɪˈliːv/
bell	/bel/
bench	/bentʃ/
best friend	/best ˈfrend/
between	/bɪˈtwiːn/
big	/bɪg/
bike	/baɪk/
bin	/bɪn/
biography	/baɪˈɒgrəfɪ/
birth ▶ date of birth	/bɜːθ, deɪt əv ˈbɜːθ/
birthday	/ˈbɜːθdeɪ/
bite	/baɪt/
black	/blæk/
blonde	/blɒnd/
blood	/blʌd/
blow	/bləʊ/
blue	/bluː/
board	/bɔːd/
boat	/bəʊt/
book	/bʊk/
bookshop	/ˈbʊkʃɒp/
border	/ˈbɔːdə(r)/
bored	/bɔːd/
boring	/ˈbɔːrɪŋ/
born ▶ was born	/bɔːn, wəz ˈbɔːn/
borrow	/ˈbɒrəʊ/
both	/bəʊθ/
bottle	/ˈbɒtl/
bough ◀ buy	/bɔːt, baɪ/
box/basket, picnic box/basket	/bɒks, ˈbɑːskɪt/ /ˈpɪknɪk bɒks, bɑːskɪt/
boy ▶ boys' school	/bɔɪ/ /ˈbɔɪz skuːl/
boyfriend	/ˈbɔɪfrend/
bracelet	/ˈbreɪslət/
bread	/bred/
break	/breɪk/
breakfast	/ˈbrekfəst/
bridge	/brɪdʒ/
brilliant	/ˈbrɪlɪənt/
Britain	/ˈbrɪtən/
brought back ◀ bring back	/brɔːt ˈbæk, brɪŋ ˈbæk/
brown	/braʊn/
brush ▶ brush teeth	/brʌʃ/ /brʌʃ ˈtiːθ/
building	/ˈbɪldɪŋ/
built ◀ build	/bɪlt/ /bɪld/
burn	/bɜːn/
burnt ◀ burn	/bɜːnt, bɜːn/
bus	/bʌs/
bus stop	/ˈbʌs stɒp/
busy	/ˈbɪzɪ/
but	/bʌt/
butcher's	/ˈbʊtʃəz/
butter	/ˈbʌtə(r)/
buy	/baɪ/
by, by 5.30	/baɪ, baɪ faɪv ˈθɜːtɪ/

C

cackle	/ˈkækl/
café	/ˈkæfeɪ/
cake	/keɪk/
call	/kɔːl/
came ◀ come	/keɪm, kʌm/
camera	/ˈkæmrə/
camp	/kæmp/
camping, go camping	/ˈkæmpɪŋ, gəʊ ˈkæmpɪŋ/
campsite	/ˈkæmpsaɪt/
can	/kæn/
Can I help you?	/kən aɪ ˈhelp juː/

Can I take a message?	/kən aɪ ˌteɪk ə ˈmesɪdʒ/
canoeing	/kəˈnuːɪŋ/
capital	/ˈkæpɪtl/
car	/kɑː(r)/
car park	/ˈkɑː pɑːk/
card	/kɑːd/
careful ▶ Be careful!	/ˈkeəfʊl, bɪ ˈkeəfʊl/
carefully	/ˈkeəfʊlɪ/
carnival	/ˈkɑːnɪvəl/
Caribbean	/ˈkærɪˈbiːən/
carrot	/ˈkærət/
carry	/ˈkærɪ/
cartoon	/kɑːˈtuːn/
cat	/kæt/
catch	/kætʃ/
cathedral	/kəˈθiːdrəl/
cave	/keɪv/
CD player	/siː ˈdiː pleɪə(r)/
celebrate	/ˈseləbreɪt/
celebration	/seləˈbreɪʃn/
cell phone (American English)	/ˈsel fəʊn/
cereal	/ˈsɪərɪəl/
champion	/ˈtʃæmpɪən/
championship	/ˈtʃæmpɪənʃɪp/
chance ▶ no chance	/tʃɑːns/ /ˈnəʊ tʃɑːns/
character	/ˈkærɪktə(r)/
charity	/ˈtʃærɪtɪ/
chat up	/tʃæt ˈʌp/
check	/tʃek/
cheek	/tʃiːk/
cheese	/tʃiːz/
cheese shop	/ˈtʃiːz ʃɒp/
chemist's	/ˈkemɪsts/
chewing gum	/ˈtʃuːɪŋ gʌm/
chicken	/ˈtʃɪkɪn/
children	/ˈtʃɪldrən/
chin	/tʃɪn/
Chinese	/tʃaɪˈniːz/
chocolate	/ˈtʃɒklət/
choose	/tʃuːz/
church, the Catholic Church	/tʃɜːtʃ/ /ðə ˈkæθlɪk tʃɜːtʃ/
cinema	/ˈsɪnəmə/
circus	/ˈsɜːkəs/
city	/ˈsɪtɪ/
clap	/klæp/
class	/klɑːs/
classroom	/ˈklɑːsruːm/
clean	/kliːn/
clever	/ˈklevə(r)/
click	/klɪk/
climb	/klaɪm/
close	/kləʊz/
clothes shop	/ˈkləʊðz ʃɒp/
cloud	/klaʊd/
cloudy	/ˈklaʊdɪ/
club	/klʌb/
coaching	/ˈkəʊtʃɪŋ/
coast	/kəʊst/
coffee	/ˈkɒfɪ/
cold ▶ It's cold.	/kəʊld/ /ɪts ˈkəʊld/
collect	/kəˈlekt/
college	/ˈkɒlɪdʒ/
comb	/kəʊm/
come	/kʌm/
come in	/kʌm ˈɪn/
comedy programme	/ˈkɒmədɪ prəʊgræm/
compass	/ˈkʌmpəs/
compass point	/ˈkʌmpəs pɔɪnt/
compete	/kəmˈpiːt/
competition	/kɒmpəˈtɪʃn/
computer	/kəmˈpjuːtə(r)/
concert	/ˈkɒnsət/
Congratulations!	/kəngrætʃʊˈleɪʃnz/
cook	/kʊk/
cookie (American English)	/ˈkʊkɪ/
cost	/ˈkɒst/
Could you say ... phoned?	/ˈkʊd juː seɪ ... ˌfəʊnd/
Could you tell me the way to ..?	/ˈkʊd juː tel miː ðə ˌweɪ tə.../

course ▶ of course	/kɔːs/ /əv ˈkɔːs/
court	/kɔːt/
cousin	/ˈkʌzn/
covers (of a bed)	/ˈkʌvəz/
crash into	/kræʃ ˈɪntə/
cricket	/ˈkrɪkɪt/
crisps	/krɪsps/
cropped	/krɒpt/
cross	/krɒs/
cuddle	/ˈkʌdl/
cupboard	/ˈkʌbəd/
curly	/ˈkɜːlɪ/
currency	/ˈkʌrənsɪ/
cycle	/ˈsaɪkl/

D
dance	/dɑːns/
dangerous	/ˈdeɪndʒərəs/
dark skinned	/dɑːk skɪnd/
dark, dark brown	/dɑːk, dɑːk ˈbraʊn/
dark, after dark	/dɑːk, ɑftə ˈdɑːk/
daughter	/ˈdɔːtə(r)/
day out	/deɪ ˈaʊt/
dear ▶ Oh dear!	/ˈdɪə(r)/ /əʊ ˈdɪə(r)/
decide	/dɪˈsaɪd/
deep	/diːp/
delicatessen	/delɪkəˈtesn/
deliver	/dɪˈlɪvə(r)/
dentist's	/ˈdentɪsts/
department store	/dɪˈpɑːtmənt stɔː(r)/
desert (n)	/ˈdezət/
designer	/dɪˈzaɪnə(r)/
desk	/desk/
detention	/dɪˈtenʃn/
devil	/ˈdevl/
diary	/ˈdaɪərɪ/
did ◀ do	/dɪd, duː/
different	/ˈdɪfrənt/
difficult	/ˈdɪfɪkəlt/
dinnertime	/ˈdɪnətaɪm/
discover	/dɪsˈkʌvə(r)/
discoverer	/dɪsˈkʌvərə(r)/
discovery	/dɪsˈkʌvərɪ/
display	/dɪsˈpleɪ/
distance	/ˈdɪstəns/
district	/ˈdɪstrɪkt/
divorce	/dɪˈvɔːs/
do well	/duː ˈwel/
doctor	/ˈdɒktə(r)/
documentary	/dɒkjʊˈmentrɪ/
doll	/dɒl/
done ▶ Well done!	/dʌn/ /wel ˈdʌn/
donkey	/ˈdɒŋkɪ/
door	/dɔː(r)/
doorway	/ˈdɔːweɪ/
doughnut	/ˈdəʊnʌt/
down	/daʊn/
dragon	/ˈdrægən/
dress	/dres/
dress up	/dres ˈʌp/
drink	/drɪŋk/
drive	/draɪv/
drop	/drɒp/
drums	/drʌmz/
dry	/draɪ/
dune	/djuːn/
during	/ˈdʒʊərɪŋ/

E
each other	/iːtʃ ˈʌðə(r)/
ear	/ɪə(r)/
early	/ˈɜːlɪ/
earn	/ɜːn/
earring	/ˈɪərɪŋ/
earth	/ɜːθ/
easily	/ˈiːzɪlɪ/
east	/iːst/

Easter	/ˈiːstə(r)/
easy	/ˈiːzɪ/
eat	/iːt/
ecology	/ɪˈkɒlədʒɪ/
education	/edʒʊˈkeɪʃn/
effects, special effects	/ɪˈfekts, speʃl ɪˈfekts/
egg	/eg/
either ... or	/ˈaɪðə(r) ... ɔː(r)/
elegant	/ˈelɪgənt/
else ? **What else?**	/els/ /wɒt ˈels/
e-mail	/ˈiː meɪl/
emperor	/ˈempərə(r)/
end ▶ in the end	/end/ /ɪn ðiː ˈend/
enemy	/ˈenəmɪ/
energetic	/enəˈdʒetɪk/
energy	/ˈenədʒɪ/
enjoy	/ɪnˈdʒɔɪ/
enough	/ɪˈnʌf/
enough ▶ **That's enough.**	/ɪˈnʌf/ /ðæts ɪˈnʌf/
episode	/ˈepɪsəʊd/
erupt	/ɪˈrʌpt/
establish	/ɪˈstæblɪʃ/
even	/ˈiːvn/
evening	/ˈiːvnɪŋ/
ever ▶ the first ever	/ˈevə(r)/ /ðə fɜːst ˈevə(r)/
every	/ˈevrɪ/
everybody	/ˈevrɪbɒdɪ/
everything	/ˈevrɪθɪŋ/
exactly	/ɪkˈzæktlɪ/
exam	/ɪkˈzæm/
excellent	/ˈeksələnt/
Excuse me.	/ɪkˈskjuːz mɪ/
exhausted	/ɪkˈzɔːstɪd/
exotic	/ɪkˈzɒtɪk/
expec ▶ I didn't expect to get a place	/ɪkˈspekt/ /aɪ dɪdnt ɪkˈspekt tə get ə pleɪs/
expensive	/ɪkˈspensɪv/
eye	/aɪ/
eyebrows	/ˈaɪbraʊz/

F

face	/feɪs/
fair skinned	/feə(r) skɪnd/
fall	/fɔːl/
fall off	/fɔːl ˈɒf/
famous	/ˈfeɪməs/
fantastic	/fænˈtæstɪk/
fast	/fɑːst/
favourite	/ˈfeɪvərɪt/
feel	/fiːl/
feet	/fiːt/
fell ◀ fall	/fel, fɔːl/
few	/fjuː/
field	/fiːld/
film	/fɪlm/
find	/faɪnd/
finger	/ˈfɪŋgə(r)/
finish	/ˈfɪnɪʃ/
finish time	/ˈfɪnɪʃ taɪm/
fire	/ˈfaɪə(r)/
fireworks	/ˈfaɪəwɜːks/
first	/fɜːst/
fish	/fɪʃ/
fishmonger	/ˈfɪʃmʌŋgə(r)/
fitness training	/ˈfɪtnəs treɪnɪŋ/
fizzy ▶ fizzy drink	/ˈfɪzɪ/ /fɪzɪ ˈdrɪŋk/
flat	/flæt/
fleece	/fliːs/
flew ◀ fly	/fluː, flaɪ/
floor	/flɔː(r)/
flour	/ˈflaʊə(r)/
fly	/flaɪ/
foggy ▶ **It's foggy.**	/ˈfɒgɪ/ /ɪts ˈfɒgɪ/
follow	/ˈfɒləʊ/
food	/fuːd/
foot	/fʊt/
football	/ˈfʊtbɔːl/
forehead	/ˈfɔːhed/

forest	/ˈfɒrɪst/
forget	/fəˈget/
Formula One	/fɔːmjʊlə ˈwʌn/
forward ▶ look forward to	/ˈfɔːwəd/ /lʊk ˈfɔːwəd tə/
found ◀ find	/faʊnd, faɪnd/
freckles	/ˈfreklz/
free time	/friː ˈtaɪm/
French fries (*American English*)	/frentʃ ˈfraɪz/
fridge	/frɪdʒ/
friend	/frend/
friendly	/ˈfrendlɪ/
frightened ▶ I'm frightened of...	/ˈfraɪtənd/ /aɪm ˈfraɪtənd əv.../
fringe	/frɪndʒ/
frozen	/ˈfrəʊzn/
fruit	/fruːt/
fruit and vegetable shop	/fruːt ən ˈvedʒtəbl ʃɒp/
fun	/fʌn/
funny	/ˈfʌnɪ/
fussy	/ˈfʌsɪ/

G

game	/geɪm/
garden	/ˈgɑːdn/
gate	/geɪt/
gave ◀ give	/geɪv, gɪv/
generous	/ˈdʒenərəs/
Geography	/dʒɒgrəfɪ/
get ▶ he gets £10	/get/ /hiː gets ten ˈpaʊndz/
get dressed	/get ˈdrest/
get off	/get ˈɒf/
get up	/get ˈʌp/
ghost	/gəʊst/
girl ▶ girls' school	/gɜːl/ /gɜːlz skuːl/
give	/gɪv/
gladiator	/ˈglædɪeɪtə(r)/
glass	/glɑːs/
glasses	/ˈglɑːsɪz/
go	/gəʊ/
go in for	/gəʊ ɪn fə(r)/
goalkeeper	/ˈgəʊlkiːpə(r)/
god	/gɒd/
Golden Jubilee	/ˌgəʊldn dʒuːbɪˈliː/
good	/gʊd/
good ▶ be good at	/gʊd/ /bɪ ˈgʊd ət/
government	/ˈgʌvənmənt/
grade ▶ A grade	/greɪd/ /ˈeɪ greɪd/
grandfather	/ˈgrænfɑːðə(r)/
grandmother	/ˈgrænmʌðə(r)/
grandparents	/ˈgrænpeərənts/
grandson	/ˈgrændsʌn/
grape	/greɪp/
great	/greɪt/
green	/griːn/
grey	/greɪ/
Guess what?	/ges ˈwɒt/
Guides	/gaɪdz/
guitar	/gɪˈtɑː(r)/

H

had ◀ have	/hæd, hæv/
hair	/heə(r)/
hairdresser's	/ˈheədresəz/
hairstyle	/ˈheəstaɪl/
Hallowe'en	/hæləʊˈiːn/
ham	/hæm/
hand	/hænd/
Hands off!	/hændz ˈɒf/
Hang on a minute!	/hæŋ ˈɒn ə mɪnɪt/
happen	/ˈhæpn/
happy ▶ He wasn't happy.	/ˈhæpɪ/ /hiː wɒznt ˈhæpɪ/
hard	/hɑːd/
hat	/hæt/
head	/hed/
head of state	/hed əv ˈsteɪt/
health	/helθ/
heard hear	/hɜːd, hɪə(r)/
heavy	/ˈhevɪ/
hell	/hel/

138

Hello, could I speak to ..., please?	/heˈləʊ, kʊd aɪ ˌspiːk tə ... pliːz/
help	/help/
help yourself	/help jɔːˈself/
helpful	/ˈhelpfʊl/
Here's your change.	/hɪəz jɔː ˈtʃeɪndʒ/
hide	/haɪd/
high	/haɪ/
hit ◀ hit	/hɪt, hɪt/
hobby	/ˈhɒbɪ/
hold onto	/həʊld ˈɒntə/
holiday	/ˈhɒlɪdeɪ/
home	/həʊm/
homework	/ˈhəʊmwɜːk/
hoot	/huːt/
hospital	/ˈhɒspɪtl/
hot ▶ It's hot.	/hɒt/ /ɪts ˈhɒt/
hour	/ˈaʊə(r)/
house	/haʊs/
How much is ... ?	/haʊ ˈmʌtʃ ɪz ... /
How's the pizza?	/ˌhaʊz ðə ˈpiːtsə/
howl	/haʊl/
huge	/hjuːdʒ/
hundred	/ˈhʌndrəd/
hungry ▶ be hungry	/ˈhʌngrɪ/ /bɪ ˈhʌngrɪ/
hurry	/ˈhʌrɪ/
hurt yourself	/ˈhɜːt jɔːself/

I

I don't care.	/aɪ dəʊnt ˈkeə(r)/
I don't know.	/aɪ dəʊnt ˈnəʊ/
I don't think so.	/aɪ dəʊnt ˈθɪŋk səʊ/
I know.	/aɪ ˈnəʊ/
I think so too.	/aɪ θɪŋk səʊ ˈtuː/
I want to ...	/aɪ wɒnt tə.../
I was only joking.	/aɪ wəz ˌəʊnlɪ ˈdʒəʊkɪŋ/
I'd like ... please.	/aɪd laɪk ...pliːz/
I'll just watch.	/aɪl dʒʌst ˈwɒtʃ/
I'm sorry, he isn't here.	/aɪm ˌsɒrɪ, hiː ɪznt ˈhɪə(r)/
ice cream	/ˈaɪs kriːm/
ice hockey	/ˈaɪs hɒkɪ/
ice skating	/ˈaɪs skeɪtɪŋ/
idea ▶ Great idea!	/aɪˈdɪə/ /ˈgreɪt aɪˌdɪə/
ill	/ɪl/
imagine	/ɪˈmædʒɪn/
independence	/ˌɪndəˈpendəns/
industrial	/ɪnˈdʌstrɪəl/
inside	/ɪnˈsaɪd/
instrument	/ˈɪnstrəmənt/
interest	/ˈɪntrest/
interesting	/ˈɪntrəstɪŋ/
international	/ˌɪntəˈnæʃnl/
internet ▶ surf the internet	/ˈɪntənet/ /sɜːf ðiː ˈɪntənet/
into	/ˈɪntə/
invite	/ɪnˈvaɪt/
Is it far?	/ɪz ɪt ˈfɑː(r)/
island	/ˈaɪlənd/
It's about a dog and a wizard.	/ɪts əbaʊt ə ˌdɒg ənd ə ˈwɪzəd/
It's fun.	/ɪts ˈfʌn/
It's lovely.	/ɪts ˈlʌvlɪ/
It's not fair.	/ɪts nɒt ˈfeə(r)/
It's not far.	/ɪts nɒt ˈfɑː(r)/
It's only a toy spider.	/ɪts ˌəʊnlɪ ə ˈtɔɪ spaɪdə(r)/
It's quite a long way.	/ɪts ˌkwaɪt ə lɒŋ ˈweɪ/
It's time for bed.	/ɪts ˌtaɪm fə ˈbed/

J

jacket	/ˈdʒækɪt/
Japanese	/ˌdʒæpəˈniːz/
jeans	/dʒiːnz/
jewel	/ˈdʒʊəl/
jeweller's	/ˈdʒʊələz/
job	/dʒɒb/
join	/dʒɔɪn/
journey	/ˈdʒɜːnɪ/
juice	/dʒuːs/
jump	/dʒʌmp/
jumper	/ˈdʒʌmpə(r)/
jungle	/ˈdʒʌŋgl/

junior	/ˈdʒuːnɪə(r)/
just	/dʒʌst/
Just then	/dʒʌst ˈðen/

K

karate	/kəˈrɑːtɪ/
kart	/kɑːt/
karting, go karting	/ˈkɑːtɪŋ, gəʊ ˈkɑːtɪŋ/
keep	/kiːp/
keep away	/kiːp əˈweɪ/
key ring	/ˈkiːrɪŋ/
kind	/kaɪnd/
king	/kɪŋ/
kit, sports kit	/kɪt, spɔːts kɪt/
kitchen	/ˈkɪtʃɪn/
kite	/kaɪt/
knee	/niː/
knock	/nɒk/
knock into	/nɒk ˈɪntə/
know ▶ you know	/nəʊ/ /juː ˈnəʊ/

L

lake	/leɪk/
lamb	/læm/
land	/lænd/
language	/ˈlæŋgwɪdʒ/
large	/lɑːdʒ/
last ▶ When did you last ...?	/lɑːst/ /ˌwen dɪd juː ˈlɑːst.../
last night	/lɑːst ˈnaɪt/
late	/leɪt/
laugh	/lɑːf/
learn	/lɜːn/
leave	/liːv/
leave on	/liːv ˈɒn/
left	/left/
left ◀ leave	/left, liːv/
left ▶ Is there much left?	/left/ /ɪz ðeə mʌtʃ ˈleft/
leg	/leg/
lemon	/ˈlemən/
let	/let/
Let's ...	/lets.../
letter	/ˈletə(r)/
licence ▶ driving licence	/ˈlaɪsəns/ /ˈdraɪvɪŋ ˌlaɪsəns/
lie	/laɪ/
life	/laɪf/
lift ▶ offer a lift	/lɪft/ /ɒfə(r) ə ˈlɪft/
light	/laɪt/
light ▶ light brown	/laɪt/ /laɪt ˈbraʊn/
lightning	/ˈlaɪtnɪŋ/
like	/laɪk/
like ▶ What ... like?	/laɪk/ /wɒt... ˈlaɪk/
lip	/lɪp/
lipstick	/ˈlɪpstɪk/
listen to	/ˈlɪsn tə/
litter	/ˈlɪtə(r)/
litter bin	/ˈlɪtə bɪn/
little	/ˈlɪtl/
little ▶ a little	/ˈlɪtl/ /ə ˈlɪtl/
living room	/ˈlɪvɪŋ ruːm/
local	/ˈləʊkl/
long	/lɒŋ/
long ▶ for long	/lɒŋ/ /fə ˈlɒŋ/
long ▶ How long ...?	/lɒŋ/ /haʊ ˈlɒŋ/
long ▶ I won't be long.	/lɒŋ/ /aɪ wəʊnt bɪ ˈlɒŋ/
look after	/lʊk ˈɑːftə(r)/
look at	/ˈlʊk ət/
look forward I'm looking forward to...	/lʊk ˈfɔːwəd/ /aɪm ˈlʊkɪŋ fɔːwəd tə.../
lose	/luːz/
lost ▶ get lost	/lɒst, get lɒst/
lot ▶ a lot of	/lɒt, ə lɒt əv/
lots of	/ˈlɒts əv/
loud	/laʊd/
love	/lʌv/
lovely	/ˈlʌvlɪ/
low	/ləʊ/
loyal	/ˈlɔɪəl/
luck	/lʌk/

lunch	/lʌntʃ/
lunchtime	/ˈlʌntʃtaɪm/

M

made ◄ make	/meɪd, meɪk/
magazine	/ˈmægəˈziːn/
magic	/ˈmædʒɪk/
mall (*American English*)	/mɔːl/
map	/mæp/
mark	/mɑːk/
market	/ˈmɑːkɪt/
marry	/ˈmærɪ/
match ▶ football match	/mætʃ/ /ˈfʊtbɔːl mætʃ/
maze	/meɪz/
meal	/miːl/
meaning	/ˈmiːnɪŋ/
meat	/miːt/
medium ▶ of medium height	/ˈmiːdɪəm/ /əv ˈmiːdɪəm haɪt/
medium length	/ˈmiːdɪəm leŋθ/
meet	/miːt/
melon	/ˈmelən/
member	/ˈmembə(r)/
mermaid	/ˈmɜːmeɪd/
mess	/mes/
microwave	/ˈmaɪkrəʊweɪv/
middle	/ˈmɪdl/
midnight	/ˈmɪdnaɪt/
mile ▶ for miles	/maɪl/ /fə ˈmaɪlz/
milk	/mɪlk/
mind ▶ **Never mind.**	/maɪnd/ /ˈnevə maɪnd/
mine	/maɪn/
minute	/ˈmɪnɪt/
miss	/mɪs/
moan	/məʊn/
mobile phone	/məʊbaɪl ˈfəʊn/
model	/ˈmɒdl/
mole	/məʊl/
moment ▶ at the moment	/ˈməʊmənt/ /ət ðə ˈməʊmənt/
monarchy	/ˈmɒnəkɪ/
money	/ˈmʌnɪ/
monster	/ˈmɒnstə(r)/
month	/mʌnθ/
monument	/ˈmɒnjʊmənt/
mood	/muːd/
moon	/muːn/
morning	/ˈmɔːnɪŋ/
most	/məʊst/
motor racing	/ˈməʊtə reɪsɪŋ/
mountain	/ˈmaʊntɪn/
mountain range	/ˈmaʊntɪn reɪndʒ/
moustache	/mʊsˈtɑːʃ/
mouth	/maʊθ/
movie theater (*American English*)	/ˈmuːvɪ θɪətə(r)/
museum	/mjuːˈzɪəm/
mushroom	/ˈmʌʃrʊm/
music	/ˈmjuːzɪk/
music programme	/ˈmjuːzɪk prəʊgræm/
music store	/ˈmjuːzɪk stɔː(r)/
musician	/mjuːˈzɪʃn/
must	/mʌst/

N

nail	/neɪl/
nature programme	/ˈneɪtʃə prəʊgræm/
naughty	/ˈnɔːtɪ/
near	/ˈnɪə(r)/
nearly	/ˈnɪəlɪ/
neat ▶ **That's neat.**	/niːt/ /ðæts ˈniːt/
neck	/nek/
necklace	/ˈnekləs/
need	/niːd/
never	/ˈnevə(r)/
new	/njuː/
New Year	/njuː ˈjɪə(r)/
news	/njuːz/
news ▶ the news	/njuːz/ /ðə ˈnjuːz/
newsagent's	/ˈnjuːzeɪdʒənts/
newspaper	/ˈnjuːspeɪpə(r)/

next	/nekst/
nice	/naɪs/
nobody	/ˈnəʊbɒdɪ/
noise	/nɔɪz/
north	/nɔːθ/
north-east	/nɔːθ ˈiːst/
north-west	/nɔːθ ˈwest/
nose	/nəʊz/
Not for me.	/nɒt fə ˈmiː/
nothing	/ˈnʌθɪŋ/
notice	/ˈnəʊtɪs/
now	/naʊ/

O

observatory	/əbˈzɜːvətrɪ/
ocean	/ˈəʊʃn/
of ▶ have a day off	/ɒf/ /hæv ə deɪ ˈɒf/
offer	/ˈɒfə(r)/
often	/ˈɒfn/
often ▶ more often	/ˈɒfn/ /mɔː(r) ˈɒfn/
Oh, I see.	/əʊ aɪ ˈsiː/
oil	/ɔɪl/
oil lamp	/ˈɔɪl læmp/
oink, oink!	/ˈɔɪŋk, ɔɪŋk/
OK	/əʊ ˈkeɪ/
old	/əʊld/
old-fashioned	/əʊld ˈfæʃnd/
Olympic Games	/əˈlɪmpɪk ˈgeɪmz/
on ▶ be on	/ɒn/ /bi ɒn/
one	/wʌn/
onion	/ˈʌnjən/
only	/ˈəʊnlɪ/
Oops!	/ʊps/
open	/ˈəʊpn/
open top bus	/əʊpn tɒp ˈbʌs/
orange	/ˈɒrɪndʒ/
organisation	/ˌɔːgənaɪˈzeɪʃn/
other	/ˈʌðə(r)/
ou ▶ be out	/aʊt/ /biː ˈaʊt/
outdoor	/ˈaʊtdɔː(r)/
outside	/aʊtˈsaɪd/
over	/ˈəʊvə(r)/
owl	/aʊl/
own ▶ on your own	/əʊn/ /ɒn jə(r) ˈəʊn/

P

pack one's bags	/pæk wʌnz ˈbægz/
pain	/peɪn/
palace	/ˈpælɪs/
pale	/peɪl/
pancake	/ˈpænkeɪk/
panther	/ˈpænθə(r)/
paper	/ˈpeɪpə(r)/
paper round, do a paper round	/ˈpeɪpə raʊnd, duː ə ˈpeɪpə raʊnd/
parade	/pəˈreɪd/
parent	/ˈpeərənt/
park the car	/pɑːk ðə kɑː(r)/
part	/pɑːt/
part ▶ take part in	/pɑːt/ /teɪk ˈpɑːt ɪn/
party	/ˈpɑːtɪ/
partying	/ˈpɑːtɪɪŋ/
pass	/pɑːs/
past	/pɑːst/
path	/pɑːθ/
patient	/ˈpeɪʃənt/
pay for	/ˈpeɪ fə(r)/
pea	/piː/
pencil case	/ˈpensɪl keɪs/
pen-friend	/ˈpenfrend/
people ▶ people say	/ˈpiːpl/ /ˈpiːpl ˈseɪ/
pepper	/ˈpepə(r)/
perform	/pəˈfɔːm/
perhaps	/pəˈhæps/
person	/ˈpɜːsən/
personal CD player	/pɜːsənl siː ˈdiː pleɪə(r)/
personality	/pɜːsəˈnælɪtɪ/
pet	/pet/

pharmacy (*American English*)	/ˈfɑːməsɪ/
phone	/fəʊn/
photo	/ˈfəʊtəʊ/
piano lesson	/pɪˈænəʊ lesn/
pick up	/pɪk ˈʌp/
picnic	/ˈpɪknɪk/
picture	/ˈpɪktʃə(r)/
piece	/piːs/
pig	/pɪg/
pink	/pɪŋk/
place	/pleɪs/
plan	/plæn/
plant	/plɑːnt/
play	/pleɪ/
play ▶ school play	/pleɪ/ /skuːl ˈpleɪ/
player	/ˈpleɪə(r)/
please	/pliːz/
plenty of	/ˈplentɪ əv/
pocket money	/ˈpɒkɪt mʌnɪ/
poetry	/ˈpəʊətrɪ/
point your toes	/pɔɪnt jə ˈtəʊz/
pointed	/ˈpɔɪntɪd /
pool	/puːl/
popular	/ˈpɒpjʊlə(r)/
population	/ˌpɒpjʊˈleɪʃn/
port	/pɔːt/
post	/pəʊst/
postcard	/ˈpəʊskɑːd/
potato	/pəˈteɪtəʊ/
potato chips (*American English*)	/pəteɪtəʊ ˈtʃɪps/
pounds	/paʊndz/
practical	/ˈpræktɪkl/
practise	/ˈpræktɪs/
present	/ˈpreznt/
prison	/prɪzn/
prize	/praɪz/
probably	/ˈprɒbəblɪ/
professional	/prəˈfeʃənl/
programme	/ˈprəʊgræm/
project	/ˈprɒdʒekt/
protect	/prəˈtekt/
Protestant	/ˈprɒtɪstənt/
proud of	/ˈpraʊd əv/
pudding ▶ Christmas pudding	/ˈpʊdɪŋ/ /krɪsməs ˈpʊdɪŋ/
pull out of	/pʊl ˈaʊt əv/
purple	/ˈpɜːpl/
purpose ▶ **You did that on purpose.**	/ˈpɜːpəs/ /juː ˌdɪd ðæt ɒn ˈpɜːpəs/
purse	/pɜːs/
push	/pʊʃ/
put	/pʊt/
put back	/pʊt ˈbæk/
put on	/pʊt ˈɒn/
put up	/pʊt ˈʌp/
pyramid	/ˈpɪrəmɪd/

Q

queen	/kwiːn/
quick	/kwɪk/
quickly	/ˈkwɪklɪ/
quiet	/ˈkwaɪət/
quietly	/ˈkwaɪətlɪ/
quite	/kwaɪt/
quiz show	/ˈkwɪz ʃəʊ/

R

race (n)	/reɪs/
race (v)	/reɪs/
racing driver	/ˈreɪsɪŋ draɪvə(r)/
rain	/reɪn/
rainforest	/ˈreɪnfɒrɪst/
raining ▶ **It's raining.**	/ˈreɪnɪŋ/ /ɪts ˈreɪnɪŋ/
raise money	/ˈreɪz ˈmʌnɪ/
read	/riːd/
ready	/ˈredɪ/
really	/ˈrɪəlɪ/
really ▶ not really	/ˈrɪəlɪ/ /nɒt ˈrɪəlɪ/

reason	/ˈriːzn/
recently	/ˈriːsəntlɪ/
record (n)	/ˈrekɔːd/
record (v)	/rɪˈkɔːd/
recycle	/riːˈsaɪkl/
red	/red/
reddish-brown	/redɪʃ ˈbraʊn/
reign	/reɪn/
relax	/rɪˈlæks/
remember	/rɪˈmembə(r)/
repeat	/rɪˈpiːt/
republic	/rɪˈpʌblɪk/
rice	/raɪs/
rich	/rɪtʃ/
ride ▶ bike ride	/raɪd/ /ˈbaɪk raɪd/
ride one's bike	/raɪd wʌnz ˈbaɪk/
right	/raɪt/
ring	/rɪŋ/
river	/ˈrɪvə(r)/
road	/rəʊd/
roller-blading	/ˈrəʊləbleɪdɪŋ/
Roman	/ˈrəʊmən/
room	/ruːm/
round	/raʊnd/
round ▶ come round	/raʊnd/ /kʌm ˈraʊnd/
round ▶ have friends round	/raʊnd/ /hæv ˈfrendz raʊnd/
roundabout	/ˈraʊndəbaʊt/
routine	/ruːˈtiːn/
routine ▶ dance routine	/ruːˈtiːn/ /ˈdɑːns ruːtiːn/
royal	/ˈrɔɪəl/
rubber	/ˈrʌbə(r)/
rugby	/ˈrʌgbɪ/
rude	/ruːd/
rules	/ruːlz/
run off with	/rʌn ˈɒf wɪð/
running, go running	/ˈrʌnɪŋ, gəʊ ˈrʌnɪŋ/

S

safe	/seɪf/
safely	/ˈseɪflɪ/
said ◀ say	/sed, seɪ/
sail	/seɪl/
salad	/ˈsæləd/
salmon	/ˈsæmən/
salt	/sɒlt/
same	/seɪm/
sand	/sænd/
sandwich	/ˈsænwɪdʒ/
sank ◀ sink	/sæŋk, sɪŋk/
sardine	/sɑːdiːn/
sausage	/ˈsɒsɪdʒ/
save	/seɪv/
saw ◀ see	/sɔː, siː/
say	/seɪ/
scar	/skɑː(r)/
science	/ˈsaɪəns/
Scotland	/ˈskɒtlənd/
Scouts	/skaʊts/
screech	/skriːtʃ/
sea	/siː/
seaside	/ˈsiːsaɪd/
see	/siː/
see ▶ **We'll see about that!**	/siː/ /wiːl ˈsiː əbaʊt ˌðæt/
seem	/siːm/
send	/send/
sen ◀ send	/sent, send/
serious	/ˈsɪərɪəs/
set off	/set ˈɒf/
shape	/ʃeɪp/
shark	/ʃɑːk/
sharp	/ʃɑːp/
ship	/ʃɪp/
shoe shop	/ˈʃuː ʃɒp/
shop	/ʃɒp/
shopping centre	/ˈʃɒpɪŋ sentə(r)/
short	/ʃɔːt/
shot up ▶ my hand shot up	/ʃɒt ˈʌp/ /maɪ ˌhænd ʃɒt ˈʌp/

should	/ʃʊd/
shoulder	/ˈʃəʊldə(r)/
show	/ʃəʊ/
shower	/ˈʃaʊə(r)/
Shrove Tuesday	/ˌʃrəʊv ˈtʃuːsdeɪ/
shy	/ʃaɪ/
sights	/saɪts/
signs	/saɪnz/
silly	/ˈsɪlɪ/
similar	/ˈsɪmɪlə(r)/
singer	/ˈsɪŋə(r)/
sink	/sɪŋk/
sit	/sɪt/
size	/saɪz/
skate	/skeɪt/
skateboard	/ˈskeɪtbɔːd/
skiing	/ˈskiːɪŋ/
skills	/skɪlz/
skin	/skɪn/
sleep	/sliːp/
slim	/slɪm/
slow	/sləʊ/
slowly	/ˈsləʊlɪ/
small	/smɔːl/
smuggler	/ˈsmʌglə(r)/
snake	/sneɪk/
sneakers (*American English*)	/ˈsniːkəz/
snow	/snəʊ/
snowboard	/ˈsnəʊbɔːd/
snowing ► (it's snowing).	/ˈsnəʊɪŋ/ /ɪts ˈsnəʊɪŋ/
snowman	/ˈsnəʊmæn/
so	/səʊ/
so ► I think so.	/səʊ/ /aɪ ˈθɪŋk səʊ/
soap opera	/ˈsəʊp ɒprə/
soccer (*American English*)	/ˈsɒkə(r)/
sofa	/ˈsəʊfə/
some	/sʌm/
someone	/ˈsʌmwʌn/
sometimes	/ˈsʌmtaɪmz/
soon	/suːn/
Sorry!	/ˈsɒrɪ/
sort ► all sorts of things	/sɔːt/ /ɔːl ˈsɔːts əv θɪŋz/
Sounds great!	/saʊndz ˈgreɪt/
soup	/suːp/
south	/saʊθ/
south-east	/saʊθ ˈiːst/
south-west	/saʊθ ˈwest/
Spanish	/ˈspænɪʃ/
speak	/spiːk/
special	/ˈspeʃl/
spend money	/spend ˈmʌnɪ/
spend time	/spend ˈtaɪm/
spicy	/ˈspaɪsɪ/
spider	/ˈspaɪdə(r)/
spiky	/ˈspaɪkɪ/
spoke ◄ speak	/spəʊk, spiːk/
sponsored	/ˈspɒnsəd/
sports programme	/ˈspɔːts prəʊgræm/
sports shop	/ˈspɔːts ʃɒp/
sporty	/ˈspɔːtɪ/
spring	/sprɪŋ/
squirt	/skwɜːt/
stand	/stænd/
stand up	/stænd ˈʌp/
star	/stɑː(r)/
star wars	/ˈstɑː wɔːz/
start	/stɑːt/
start time	/stɑːt taɪm/
statue	/ˈstætʃuː/
stay	/steɪ/
stay ► have friends to stay	/steɪ/ /hæv ˈfrendz tə steɪ/
stay over	/steɪ ˈəʊvə(r)/
stay up	/steɪ ˈʌp/
steam boat	/ˈstiːm bəʊt/
step	/step/
step ► dance steps	/step/ /ˈdɑːns steps/
stick	/stɪk/
sticker	/ˈstɪkə(r)/

still	/stɪl/
stomach	/ˈstʌmək/
stop	/stɒp/
Stop it!	/ˈstɒp ɪt/
storm	/stɔːm/
story	/ˈstɔːrɪ/
straight	/streɪt/
Straight after lunch.	/ˌstreɪt ɑːftə ˈlʌntʃ/
straight on	/streɪt ˈɒn/
strange	/streɪndʒ/
strap	/stræp/
street	/striːt/
strict	/strɪkt/
strong	/strɒŋ/
studio	/ˈstjuːdɪəʊ/
study	/ˈstʌdɪ/
style	/staɪl/
stylish	/ˈstaɪlɪʃ/
subject	/ˈsʌbdʒɪkt/
suddenly	/ˈsʌdnlɪ/
sugar	/ˈʃʊgə(r)/
suitcase	/ˈsuːtkeɪs/
summer	/ˈsʌmə(r)/
sun	/sʌn/
sunglasses	/ˈsʌnglɑːsɪz/
sunny ► It's sunny.	/ˈsʌnɪ/ /ɪts ˈsʌnɪ/
sunscreen	/ˈsʌnskriːn/
supermarket	/ˈsuːpəmɑːkɪt/
superstar	/ˈsuːpəstɑː(r)/
supper	/ˈsʌpə(r)/
sure	/ʃʊə(r)/
surf	/sɜːf/
surfboard	/ˈsɜːfbɔːd/
surprise	/səˈpraɪz/
sweater (*American English*)	/ˈswetə(r)/
sweatshirt	/ˈswetʃɜːt/
sweets	/swiːts/
swimming	/ˈswɪmɪŋ/
swimsuit	/ˈswɪmsuːt/
swing	/swɪŋ/
switch off	/swɪtʃ ˈɒf/

T

take	/teɪk/
take ► It takes an hour.	/teɪk/ /ɪt teɪks ən ˈaʊə(r)/
talent show	/ˈtælənt ʃəʊ/
talk	/tɔːk/
tall	/tɔːl/
tall ► How tall are you?	/tɔːl/ /haʊ ˈtɔːl ə juː/
tea	/tiː/
team	/tiːm/
teenager	/ˈtiːneɪdʒə(r)/
teeth	/tiːθ/
television	/ˈteləvɪʒn/
temple	/ˈtempl/
tennis	/ˈtenɪs/
tent	/tent/
than	/ðæn/
Thanks.	/θæŋks/
that	/ðæt/
That's £1.99 please.	/ðæts ˈwʌn naɪntɪ ˌnaɪn pliːz/
That's why ...	/ˈðæts waɪ.../
theatre	/ˈθɪət ə(r)/
theme park	/ˈθiːm pɑːk/
then	/ðen/
thin	/θɪn/
thing	/θɪŋ/
think	/θɪŋk/
think of	/θɪŋk əv/
thirsty, be thirsty	/ˈθɜːstɪ, bɪ θɜːstɪ/
this	/ðɪs/
thought ◄ think	/θɔːt, θɪŋk/
thousand	/ˈθaʊzənd/
threw ◄ throw	/θruː, θrəʊ/
through ► through the streets	/θruː/ /θruː ðə ˈstriːts/
throw	/θrəʊ/
thunder	/ˈθʌndə(r)/
ticket	/ˈtɪkɪt/

tidy	/ˈtaɪdɪ/
tiger	/ˈtaɪɡə(r)/
tight	/taɪt/
till	/tɪl/
time	/taɪm/
time ▶ have a good time	/taɪm/ /hæv ə ɡʊd ˈtaɪm/
times	/taɪmz/
tired	/ˈtaɪəd/
tip	/tɪp/
tobacco	/təˈbækəʊ/
toe	/təʊ/
together	/təˈɡeðə(r)/
tomato	/təˈmɑːtəʊ/
tomorrow	/təˈmɒrəʊ/
tongue	/tʌŋ/
tonight	/təˈnaɪt/
too	/tuː/
took ◀ take	/tʊk, teɪk/
tooth	/tuːθ/
top	/tɒp/
toss	/tɒs/
touch	/tʌtʃ/
tour ▶ on tour	/ˈtʊə(r)/ /ɒn ˈtʊə(r)/
tourist features	/ˈtʊərɪst fiːtʃəz/
towards	/təˈwɔːdz/
town ▶ go into town	/taʊn/ /ɡəʊ ɪntə ˈtaʊn/
track	/træk/
track ▶ karting track	/træk/ /ˈkɑːtɪŋ træk/
trail, treasure trail	/treɪl/ /ˈtreʒə treɪl/
train	/treɪn/
trainers	/ˈtreɪnəz/
travel	/ˈtrævl/
trick	/trɪk/
trip	/trɪp/
trouble ▶ get into trouble	/ˈtrʌbl/ /ɡet ɪntə ˈtrʌbl/
true	/truː/
try	/traɪ/
T-shirt	/ˈtiː ʃɜːt/
tummy	/ˈtʌmɪ/
tuna	/ˈtʃuːnə/
turkey	/ˈtɜːkɪ/
turn	/tɜːn/
turn off	/tɜːn ˈɒf/
turning	/ˈtɜːnɪŋ/
TV	/tiː ˈviː/

U

ugly	/ˈʌɡlɪ/
Ugh!	/ʌɡ/
UK	/juː ˈkeɪ/
umbrella	/ʌmˈbrelə/
uncle	/ˈʌŋkl/
under	/ˈʌndə(r)/
understand	/ʌndəˈstænd/
uniform	/ˈjuːnɪfɔːm/
United States	/juːnaɪtɪd ˈsteɪts/
until	/ənˈtɪl/
up	/ʌp/
us	/ʌs/
use	/juːz/
usual	/ˈjuːʒʊəl/
usually	/ˈjuːʒəlɪ/

V

Valentine's Day	/ˈvæləntaɪnz deɪ/
vegetables	/ˈvedʒtəblz/
very	/ˈverɪ/
view	/vjuː/
vinegar	/ˈvɪnɪɡə(r)/
visit	/ˈvɪzɪt/
voice	/vɔɪs/
volcano	/vɒlˈkeɪnəʊ/

W

wait	/weɪt/
wake up ▶ She wakes me up.	/weɪk ˈʌp/ /ʃɪ weɪks miː ˈʌp/
Wales	/weɪlz/

walk (n.)	/wɔːk/
walk (v.)	/wɔːk/
wall	/wɔːl/
wallet	/ˈwɒlɪt/
walls	/wɔːlz/
want	/wɒnt/
warm ▶ It's warm.	/wɔːm/ /ɪts ˈwɔːm/
washing-up ▶ do the washing-up	/wɒʃɪŋ ˈʌp/ /duː ðə wɒʃɪŋ ˈʌp/
waste	/weɪst/
watch (n.)	/wɒtʃ/
watch (v.)	/wɒtʃ/
Watch out!	/wɒtʃ ˈaʊt/
water	/ˈwɔːtə(r)/
water pistol	/ˈwɔːtə pɪstəl/
water sports	/ˈwɔːtə spɔːts/
waterfall	/ˈwɔːtəfɔːl/
wavy	/ˈweɪvɪ/
way ▶ a long way	/weɪ/ /ə lɒŋ ˈweɪ/
wear	/weə(r)/
weather	/ˈweðə(r)/
weather ▶ the weather	/ˈweðə(r)/ /ðə ˈweðə(r)/
We'll meet in the usual place.	/wiːl miːt ɪn ðə juːʒʊəl ˈpleɪs/
week	/wiːk/
weekend	/ˈwiːkend/
We got into a lot of trouble.	/wiː ɡɒt ɪntʊ ə lɒt əv ˈtrʌbl/
welcome	/ˈwelkəm/
well	/wel/
Welsh	/welʃ/
went ◀ go	/went, ɡəʊ/
west	/west/
wetsuit	/ˈwetsuːt/
what?	/wɒt/
When is … on?	/wen ɪz … ɒn/
where?	/weə(r)/
which?	/wɪtʃ/
whistle	/ˈwɪsl/
white	/waɪt/
who?	/huː/
whose?	/huːz/
Why don't we …?	/waɪ dəʊnt wiː…/
why?	/waɪ/
wife	/waɪf/
Will you be out for long?	/wɪl juː biː aʊt fə ˈlɒŋ/
win	/wɪn/
wind	/wɪnd/
window	/ˈwɪndəʊ/
windy ? It's windy.	/ˈwɪndɪ/ /ɪts ˈwɪndɪ/
wing	/wɪŋ/
winner	/ˈwɪnə(r)/
winter	/ˈwɪntə(r)/
wish	/wɪʃ/
witch	/wɪtʃ/
with	/wɪð/
woman	/ˈwʊmən/
work	/wɜːk/
worksheet	/ˈwɜːkʃiːt/
world	/wɜːld/
World Cup	/wɜːld ˈkʌp/
worry ▶ Don't worry.	/ˈwɒrɪ/ /dəʊnt ˈwɒrɪ/
Would you like to …?	/wʊd juː laɪk tə…/
wrist	/rɪst/
wrong ▶ do something wrong	/rɒŋ/ /duː sʌmθɪŋ ˈrɒŋ/
wrote ◀ write	/rəʊt, raɪt/

Y

year	/jɪə(r)/
Yes, hold on, I'll get her for you.	/jes, həʊld ɒn, aɪl get hə fə juː/
young	/jʌŋ/
Yuck!	/jʌk/

Z

zoo	/zuː/

Macmillan Education
Between Towns Road, Oxford, OX4 3PP
A division of Macmillan Publishers Limited
Companies and representatives throughout the world.

ISBN 1 405 01907 7

© Christopher Barker and Libby Mitchell 2005
Design and illustration © Macmillan Publishers 2005

First published 2005

All rights reserved; no parts of this publication may be reproduced, stored in a retrieval system, transmitted in any form, or by any means, electronic, mechanical, photocopying, recording, or otherwise, without the prior written permission of the publishers.

Designed by Mackerel Limited.
Illustrated by Mark Davis.
Cover design by Mackerel Limited.
Cover photo by Getty.

The authors and publishers would like to thank the following for permission to reproduce their material:

Reach Words and Music by Cathy Dennis and Andrew Todd copyright © EMI Music Publishing Ltd and BMG Music Publishing Ltd (50%) EMI Music Publishing Ltd, London, WC2H 0QY 1999, reprinted by permission of International Music Publications Ltd and Music Sales Limited. All Rights Reserved.

Lady (Hear Me Tonight) Words and Music by Romain Tranchart, Yann Destagnol, Nile Rodgers and Bernard Edwards copyright © Universal Music Publishing Ltd, Bernard's Other Music and Sony Music International UK (25%) Warner/Chappell Music Ltd, London, W6 8BS 2000, reprinted by permission of International Music Publications Ltd and Music Sales Ltd. All Rights Reserved.

Commissioned photography by Haddon Davies pp 6/7, 8, 10, 12, 14, 15, 20, 22, 23, 32, 34, 38, 44(b), 46, 48, 56, 58, 60, 62, 68, 70, 72, 76(tl,br), 82/3, 84, 86, 92/3, 94, 104(b), 106, 108, 110, 116, 119, 121

Picture Research by Pippa McNee.

The authors and publishers would like to thank the following for permission to reproduce photographs their photographic material:

Alamy pp28 (t), 29(b), 53(t), 59(m), 100(b), 124(tl, mr ml); Andes Press Agency p40 (l); Anglia Press / Warren Page, pp64, 65; Anthony Blake pp61 (t), 88(t), 131 Corbis pp44 (t), 52(m. bl. br), 53(m), 59(b), 100(tl, tr), 124(br, bl); Eye ubiquitous pp26, 28(b), 29(t), 36(3), 50, 131(b); Guide Association p76 (br, tl); Historical Royal Palaces p93 (background only); Image Bank pp41 (b), 128(t); Japanese Embassy pp88 (m, b), 89; Panos Pictures p41 (t); Redferns pp104 (t), 118(t), 122, 133, 134; Rex Features / Luca Films – Press shot pp74 75; Stone pp49, 52(t), 53(b), and 125, 132; Taxi p361, 2, 4), 40(r), 59(t), 61(b), 124(TR), 128(b).

Comissioned Photography by Haddon Davies pp6, 7, 8, 10, 12, 20, 22, 23, 24, 32, 34, 35, 38, 44(b), 46, 48, 56, 58, 60, 62, 68, 70, 72, 76(tl, br), 80, 82, 83, 84, 86, 92, 93, 94, 104(b), 106, 108, 110, 116, 118(b), 119, 120, 121.

The publishers wish to thank the following; Dominic Barklem, Kim Calder-Smith, Alexander Green, Gabor Herendi, Aimee Kotowicz, Alexandra Morris, James Wilson, Max Pearmain, Borders, Oxford; Elmer Cotton Sports, Oxford; Chris Durham and all at The Theatre, Chipping Norton; Diana Meadowcroft and family, Sarah Meadows, all the staff at Oxford Museum, Woodstock; RUDA Holiday Park, Croyde; Nick Smith, Sylvester, Oxford, Thames Trains Ltd.

And a very special thank you to our Development Editor, Daniela Morini, and our Publisher, Emma Byrne, whose commitment and enthusiasm have contributed so much to this project.

Printed and bound in Spain by Edelvives
2009   2008   2007   2006   2005